SCUNTHORPE TO DONCASTER

Vic Mitchell & Keith Smith

Vic Mitchell

Keith Smith

MP Middleton Press

Front cover: No. 56038 hauls empty wagons over the spectacular Keadby Bascule Bridge in July 1987, while the northern part of it supports three vehicles running towards Althorpe station on the A18. (J.D.Cable/Colour-Rail.com)

Back cover upper: Two brake vans were provided to convey a group of railway students on 13th August 1960 to Epworth, behind 2-6-0 no. 46407. This Light Railway had very low platforms provided. One photographer is bottom-up. The windmill needed wind. (B.Hilton/Colour-Rail.com)

Back cover lower: The 1947 Railway Clearing House map has the main route across it and the branches vertically.

ACKNOWLEDGEMENTS

We are very grateful for the assistance received from many of those mentioned in the credits, also from R.S.Carpenter, A.J.Castledine, G.Croughton, G.Gartside, R.Geach, J.Hinson (Signalling Record Society), C.M.Howard, N.Langridge, B.Lewis, D. and Dr S. Salter, T.Walsh and, in particular, our always supportive families.

Published August 2019

ISBN 978 1 910356 34 0

© *Middleton Press, 2019*

Production & Cover design Deborah Esher
Typesetting & Design Cassandra Morgan

Published by
　　　Middleton Press
　　　Easebourne Lane
　　　Midhurst
　　　West Sussex
　　　GU29 9AZ
Tel: 01730 813169
Email: info@middletonpress.co.uk
www.middletonpress.co.uk

Printed and bound by CPI Group (UK) Ltd, Croydon, CR0 4YY

CONTENTS

INDEX

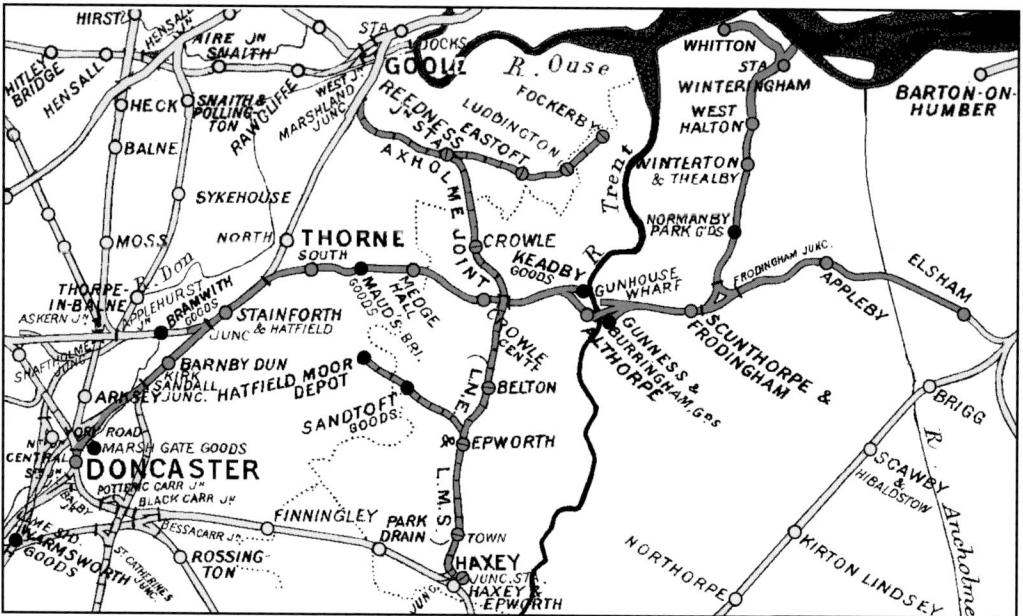

1. The 1947 Railway Clearing House map is the basis of this album, but many of the lines were goods only by that time. The routes featured in this volume are shown in grey. Just beyond the right border is Barnetby station, which still offers trains on the three routes radiating from Wrawby Junction, which is on the right border. The curved line can be found in our *Lincoln to Cleethorpes* album. The one from Brigg is featured in *Gainsborough to Sheffield*.

GEOGRAPHICAL SETTING

We will consider the geological outcrops in journey order, which is mainly east to west. The mineral bands are from north to south and we begin at Elsham on red sandstones. They are narrow bands and we soon move onto a small ridge of limestone. Extensive sandstone follows and both of these have been of great commercial importance. The latter was particularly so, owing to its ironstone content, which eventually gave rise to the massive steelworks of the district.

The Old River Ancholme and the almost straight New River Ancholme flow north under the first part of our route. After leaving Scunthorpe, the line passes over the north-flowing River Trent. Joining this nearby is the New Idle River and there are several Drains, with names which relate to this almost flat landscape.

The Isle of Axholme reaches 87ft above sea level and was once a true island, before the drainage systems were completed. The Romans established Doncaster on ground rising on the east side of the north-flowing River Don. All the rivers mentioned above flow into the Humber, where the Whitton branch terminated.

Most of the routes herein were in Lincolnshire; only the lines west of Thorne were built in Yorkshire.

The maps are to the scale of 12ins to 1 mile, with north at the top, unless otherwise indicated.

HISTORICAL BACKGROUND

Main Lines

Doncaster received the Great Northern Railway from the north in 1848 and its extension southwards in 1849. Also that year was the completion of the South Yorkshire, Doncaster & Goole line from the west. In the next year, its name became the South Yorkshire & River Dun Navigation Railway. The line was extended east through Scunthorpe to Barnetby by the Trent, Ancholme & Grimsby Railway on 1st October 1866. Here it joined the 1848 route of the Manchester, Sheffield and Lincolnshire Railway. This was renamed the Great Central Railway in 1897, the TA&GR having joined the MS&LR in 1882. The GCR became a large part of the London & North Eastern Railway in 1923 and thus the Eastern Region of British Railways in 1948. A new station opened at Kirk Sandall, north of Doncaster on 13th May 1991.

Under privatisation, all services were operated by Regional Railways North East from 2nd March 1997 and were re-branded as Northern Spirit in May 1998. This became Arriva Trains Northern from 27th April 2001. As part of a remapping of services in the north of England, two new franchises were designed and let. A new TransPennine Express franchise was created on 1st February 2004, operated by First-Keolis. This was replaced by another TransPennine Express franchise on 1st April 2016, run by First. It operated an hourly fast service between Cleethorpes

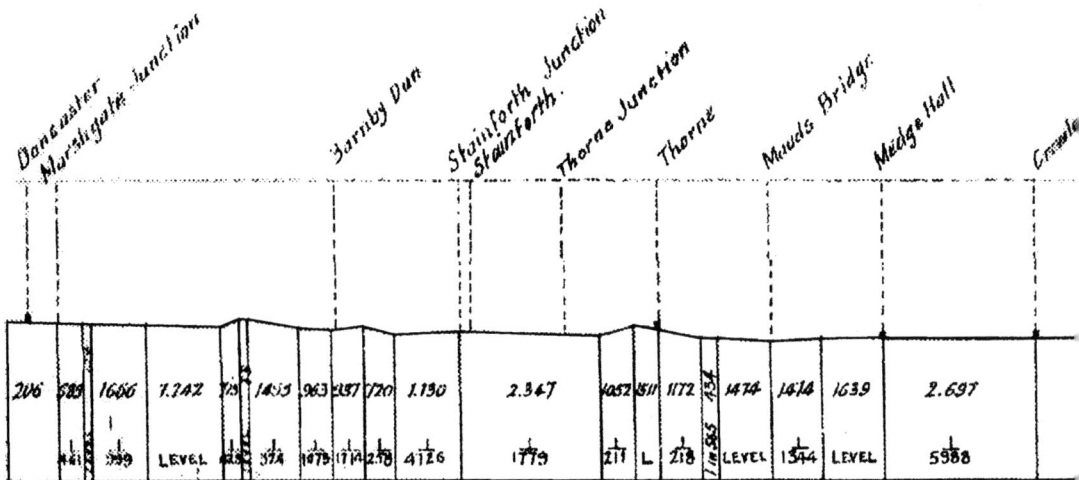

and Manchester Airport. A new Northern franchise was also created on 12th December 2004, operated by Serco-Abellio. This was replaced by another new Northern franchise on 1st April 2016, run by Arriva. It operated an hourly stopping service between Scunthorpe and Doncaster. At the western end of the route, it also operated two trains an hour between Hull and Sheffield, some of which started back from Bridlington or Scarborough.

Axholme Joint Railway

This was built as a joint enterprise of the North Eastern and Lancashire & Yorkshire Railways mainly for agricultural produce. The Axholme Joint Railway was an amalgamation of the Goole & Marshland Railway (built in 1898-1903) and Isle of Axholme Light Railway companies.

The AJR opened the Fockerby to Crowle section on 10th August 1903 and the Crowle to Haxey Junction section on 2nd January 1905. The line passed into LNER and LMSR joint ownership at the grouping in 1923. Passenger services ceased on 17th July 1933.

The Haxey Junction to Epworth section closed in 1956, the Hatfield Moor Branch closed in 1964 and the remainder closed on 5th April 1965. However, most of the track was retained and operated as a long siding. This allowed it to be used to carry heavy parts from Keadby Power Station across the Stainforth & Keadby Canal, as the bridge on the A161 could not support their weight. The road bridge was replaced in 1970, and the rails were removed in 1972.

The branch to Hatfield Moor ran west from Epworth and was for goods only. It was built in 1907-08 as a Light Railway. It was opened on 1st March 1909 and carried peat from about 1913. Closure came on 29th February 1964.

North Lindsey Light Railway

Incorporated in 1900, the first five miles from its own station in Dawes Lane, Scunthorpe, to Winterton & Thealby, was opened on 3rd September 1906. It was worked by the GCR. The extension to Winteringham was opened on 13th July 1907, the first train carrying 254 passengers. The final 2½ miles from Winteringham to Whitton was opened on 1st December 1910. The branch was single line from Normanby Park North signal box (just outside Scunthorpe) to Whitton, and served wharves at Winteringham.

Passenger services were withdrawn on 13th July 1925. However, the line carried a heavy mineral traffic during World War II and freight facilities were not withdrawn until 1st October 1951 from Whitton and Winteringham, 29th May 1961 from West Halton and 20th July 1964 from Winterton & Thealby, though this last section, from Frodingham Junction to Winterton & Thealby was also open for sidings traffic until 20th June 1964. The remainder was still in use in 2019 for spoil and commercial waste.

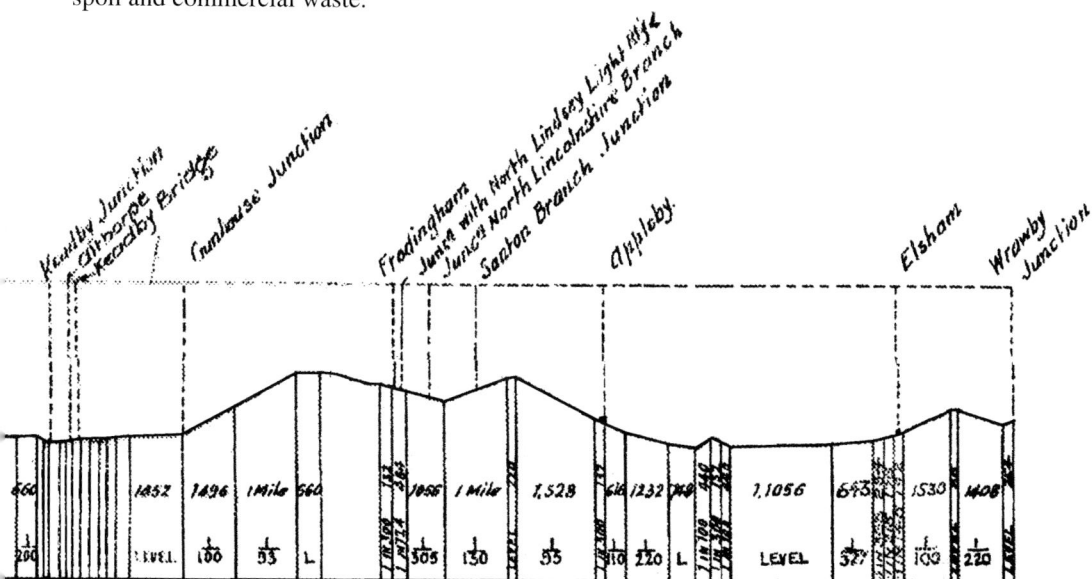

PASSENGER SERVICES

Main Line

The table below shows figures for trains running on at least five days per week. Most trains have operated from Cleethorpes and/or Grimsby to Doncaster. The sample timetables reveal that the majority have called at all stations.

	Stopping		Fast	
	Weekdays	Sundays	Weekdays	Sundays
1869	3	0	-	-
1895	5	0	-	-
1921	8	2	2	0
1953	7	3	0	0
1991	15	0	0	9

Initially, there were a few extra trains to Doncaster starting at Keadby, on the west bank of the Trent. They ceased in 1874.

Recently, Scunthorpe has had an hourly stopping train from Cleethorpes, which continued non-stop to Doncaster and beyond. A stopping service to Doncaster started at Scunthorpe every hour. This relates to weekdays. On Sundays, hourly through trains were on offer, but they did not stop between Scunthorpe and Doncaster.

December 1895   June 1869 ↗

CLEETHORPES, GRIMSBY, HULL, GOOLE, DONCASTER, BARNSLEY, and PENISTONE.—Manchester, Sheffield, and Lincolnshire.

Miles from Penistone.	Up.	Week Days.							Sundays.		
	Alexandra Bldngs., Jas. St.,	mrn	mrn	c	mrn	aft	aft	aft	mrn	aft	aft
	199 Liverpool (per' bus) dep	....	....	8 15	1015	1 25	3 5	4 45	....	....	3 0
	199 ,, Brunswck Sta. ,,	....	....	8 30	1030	1 40	3 20	5 0	....	....	3 15
	192 Manchester (Lon.R.) ,,	....	6 45	10 0	1145	3 0	5 0	6 30	7 0	3 30	5 0
	194 Sheffield (Victoria) ,,	....	6 15	9 50	1230	2 35	4 40	6¼6½	7 20	....	7 40
—	Penistone dep	....	7 45	1055	1 5	3 55	5 55	8 5	8 34	5 5	8 25
3¾	Silkstone	....	7 54	11 4	1 15	4 4	6 4	8 15	8 44	5 15	8 35
5½	Dodworth	....	8 0	1110	1 21	4 10	6 10	8 21	8 50	5 24	8 42
—	Summer Lane	....	8 5	....	1 27	4 15	b	8 27	8 57	5 31	8 51
7¾	Barnsley 205 arr	....	8 8	1118	1 30	4 18	6 18	8 30	9 0	5 34	8 55
	dep	....	8 13	1120	☞	4 23	6 20	8 35	9 4	5 40	9 0
10	Ardsley	....	8 19	....	Stop	4 29	...	....	9 10	5 46	9 6
—	190 Sheffield (Victoria) dep	....	7 25	1025	....	3 15	5 25	....	8 15	5 0	....
12½	Wombwell	....	8 26	1131	....	4 37	6 34	8 46	9 18	5 55	9 15
15	Wath	....	8 32	1137	....	4 43	6 41	8 54	9 24	6 3	9 23
17	Mexbro' Junction 176	....	8 39	1143	....	4 50	6 48	9 0	9 30	6 12	9 30
19½	Conisbro'	....	8 47	1149	1&2	5 0	6 58		9 38	6 21	
22	Sprotbro'	....	f	bk	gov	f	b		9 44	6 28	
24½	Doncaster 102, 101, 205, 104, 108, 109 arr	....	9 0	12 0	aft	5 10	7 8		9 50	6 35	
	dep	....	9 35	1210	4 10	5 15	7 15				
29	Barnby Dun	....	9 46	1221	4 24	5 26	7 26				
31½	Stainforth and Hatfield	....	9 52	1227	4 32	5 32	7 32				
34½	Thorne, for Newbridg & Goole	....	10 0	1235	4 41	5 40	7 40				
37½	Medge Hall	....	....	....	4 53	....	....				
38½	Godnow Bridge	1,2,3	....	....	4 58	....	....				
40½	Crowle, for Epworth & Belton	gov	1017	1252	5 5	5 57	7 57				
—	Keadby, for Amcotts & Burringham	mrn	....	1 0	5 15	....	8 5				
43½	Althorpe	9 0	1027	....		6 8	....				
48	Frodingham	9 12	1039	....		6 19	....				
51¼	Appleby	9 20	1046	....		6 26	....				
56	Elsham	9 32	1058	....		6 39	....				
58½	Barnetby 198 *and above* arr	9 40	11 3	....		6 45	....				
—	Hull (*see table above*) arr	1055	1215	....		....	....				
—	Barnetby dep	Tues. & Fri. only	11 5	...		6 47	....				
63¼	Brocklesby		....	....		6 57	....				
66½	Habrough		1120	....		7 4	....				
70	Stallingbro'		1130	....		7 14	....				
72½	Great Coates		1135	....		7 19	....				
74½	Grimsby 195 Town arr		1140	....		7 25	....				
	Docks ,,		1150	....		7 35	....				
77½	Cleethorpes ,,		1158	....		8 12	....				

☞ Saturdays only Doncaster to Keadby.

c Stop to set down on notice being given to the Guard at Grimsby.

k Stops to take up for Doncaster on Saturdays

f Stop to take up for Stations beyond Keadby.

c 3rd class from Liverpool to South Yorkshire Stations.

Down.	Week Days.									Sundays.			
	mrn	a	mrn	d	aft	aft	aft	aft	aft	mrn	mrn	aft	aft
Cleethorpes dep				8 50	....	2 30	4 40	....	....				
Grimsby Docks ,,				9 0	....	2 38	4 48	....	....				
Grimsby Town ,,				9 20	....	2 45	5 5	....	....				
Great Coates				[illegible]	....	....	5 11	....	....				
Stallingbro'				[illegible]		....	5 17	....	....				
Habrough				9 42		....	5 26	....	....				
Brocklesby				9 48		c	....	....	....				
Barnetby arr				9 58		3 14	....	....	....				
Hull 194 dep				8g10		2 15	5 0	....	....				
Barnetby dep				10 0		3 25	6 10	....	....				
Elsham				10 6		3 32	6 17	....	....				
Appleby				1017		3 41	6 29	....	....				
Frodingham				1026		3 56	6 41	....	....				
Althorpe [ringham				1040		4 10	6 55	....	....				
Keadby, for Amcotts & Bur-		7 5	9 0	....		....		7 25					
Crowle, for Epworth & Belton		7 13	9 10	1048		4 23		7 33					
Godnow Bridge		....	9 15	....		....		....					
Medge Hall		....	9 20	....		....		....					
Thorne, for Newbdge & Goole		7 30	9 35	11 0		4 42		7 52					
Stainforth and Hatfield		7 38	9 45	11 7		4 51		8 1					
Barnby Dun		7 44	9 55	1113		5 0		8 10					
Doncaster 102, 101, 205, 104, 108, 109 arr		7 55	1010	1125		5 15		8 23					
dp		8 10	☞	1136	3 50	5 40		8 35			10 0		6 45
Sprotbro'		b	Stop	j	....	b		b		1,2,3	10 6		6 51
Conisbro'		8 21	....	1146	4 0	5 51		8 44		gov	1012		6 58
Mexbro' Junction 176		8 28	....	1153	4 6	5 58		8 50		6 50	1019		7 5
Wath		8 34	....	1159	4 12	6 4		8 57		6 55	1025		7 13
Wombwell		8 41	....	12 6	4 18	6 10		9 4		7 4	1032		7 22
190 Sheffield (Victoria) arr	....	9 55	....	1 5	....	7 20		10 0		....	1125		8 25
Ardsley	1,2,3	8 49	1&2	1&2	....	....		9 12		7 11	1039		7 29
Barnsley 205 arr	gov	8 57	aft	1216	4 29	6 23		9 20		7 17	1045		7 35
dep	6 15	9 0	2 30	1221	4 32	6 25		....	9 30	7 20	....	4 25	7 40
Summer Lane	6 18	b	2 33	1224	4 35	6 28		....	9 33	7 23	....	4 28	7 43
Dodworth	6 24	9 9	2 39	1230	4 41	6 34		....	9 39	7 30	....	4 35	7 50
Silkstone	6 30	9 15	2 45	1236	4 47	6 40		....	9 45	7 38	....	4 43	7 58
Penistone 192, 194, 191 arr	6 40	9 25	2 55	1246	4 57	6 50		....	9 55	7 50	....	4 55	8 8
192 Sheffield (Victoria) arr	8 10	1045	3 55	1 23	5 57	8 35		....	1040	9 5	....	5 35	....
195 Manchester (L. Rd.) ,,	8 22	1040	4 30	2 10	6 0	7 55		....	....	9 30	....	7 50	9 45
199 Liverpool, Brunswck ,,	9 51	12 5	....	4 20	7 25	9 21		....	....	1157	....	....	1125
199 ,, James Street ,,	10 5	1220	....	4 35	7 40	9 35		....	....	1210	....	....	1140

b Stop to take up or set down when required.

g Passengers from Hull change at Habrough.

j Stops to set down from Stations beyond Keadby.

Saturdays only ☞ Keadby to Doncaster.

d 3rd class from Barnsley to Manchester.

☞ Tuesdays and Fridays only.

Saturdays only.

a 1&2 class only between Barnsley and Penistone.

k Stop to take up when required.

☞ All Trains are 1 & 3 gov. on South Yorkshire Line.

1 3rd class to Liverpool from Stations between Keadby and Ardsley inclusive.

Axholme Joint Railway

Goole to Haxey Junction had three trains initially, with connections to Fockerby at Reedness Junction. These were soon reduced to two. There were never any on Sundays. Fockerby lost its Saturday trains in 1906. The services were minimal and two examples are shown. World War I and the 1926 General Strike brought prolonged gaps and bad publicity.

July 1904

GOOLE, REEDNESS JUNCTION FOCKERBY and CROWLE.—Axholme Joint.

Mls		mrn	mrn	Weds. and Sats. aft	aft
—	Goole dep.	....	9 50	1245	5 45
7¾	Reedness Junction arr.	....	10 3	1259	5 58
—	Reedness Junction dep.	....	1031	1 1	6 26
10¾	Eastoft	....	1040	1 10	6 35
12	Luddington	....	1044	1 14	6 39
13½	Fockerby arr.	....	1048	1 18	6 43
—	Reedness Junction dep.	8 42	10 4	1 0	5 59
10¾	Crowle 624, 625 arr.	8 51	1013	1 9	6 8

Mls		mrn	mrn	Weds. and Sats. aft	aft
—	Crowle dep.	8 55	1017	1 35	6 12
3	Reedness Junction arr.	9 4	1026	1 44	6 21
Mls	Fockerby dep.	8 20	....	1 29	6 47
1¼	Luddington	8 24	...	1 33	6 51
2½	Eastoft	8 28	....	1 37	6 55
5¼	Reedness Junction arr.	8 37	....	1 46	7 4
—	Reedness Junction dep.	9 5	....	1 50	7 5
10¾	Goole 570, 637 (*and side*) arr	9 18	....	2 3	7 18

April 1932

GOOLE, FOCKERBY, CROWLE, and HAXEY JUNCTION (**One class only**).—L.M.&S. and L.&N.E.

Miles.	Down.	Week Days only.						
		mrn	mrn S		aft B	aft S	aft E	aft S
	Goole dep.	6 45	9 32	..	1218	3 7	5 25	5 45
5¾	Reedness Junction .. arr.	6 57	9 44	....	1230	3 19	5 37	5 57
—	Reedness Junction dep.	..	..	..	..	..	5 41	..
8¾	Eastoft	....	....	....	....	....	5 50	....
10	Luddington	..	..	..	..	..	5 54	..
11½	Fockerby arr.	....	....	....	....	....	5 58	....
—	Reedness Junction .. dep.	6 58	9 45	..	1232	3 20	5 39	5 59
8¾	Crowle 905, 911 .. arr.	7 6	9 53	....	1240	3 28	5 47	6 7
	dep.	7 7	9 54	..	1241	3 29	5 48	6 8
13	Belton	7 19	10 6	....	1253	3 41	6 0	6 20
14¾	Epworth	7 25	1012	..	1259	3 47	6 6	6 26
17¾	Haxey Town	7 33	1020	....	1 7	3 55	6 14	6 34
19½	Haxey Junc. 892, 893 ar.	7 37	1024	..	1 11	3 59	6 18	6 38

Miles.	Up.	Week Days only.							
		mrn	mrn S		aft B	aft S	aft E	aft S	
	Haxey Junction .... dep.	8 0	1050	..	1 30	4 15	6 50	7 20	..
1¾	Haxey Town	8 5	1055	....	1 35	4 20	6 55	7 25	....
4¾	Epworth	8 15	11 4	..	1 43	4 28	7 3	7 33	..
6½	Belton	8 22	1112	....	1 50	4 35	7 10	7 40	....
10¾	Crowle 905, 911 .. arr.	8 33	1124	..	2 1	4 46	7 21	7 51	..
	dep.	8 34	1125	....	2 2	4 47	7 22	7 52	....
13¾	Reedness Junction .. arr.	8 42	1133	..	2 10	4 55	7 30	8 0	..
—	Mls Fockerby dep.	8E25	....	....	....	....	6 20	....	....
—	1¼ Luddington	8E29	..	..	..	..	6 24	..	..
—	2½ Eastoft	8E33	....	....	....	....	6 28	....	....
—	5¼ Reedness Junc.. arr.	8E42	..	..	..	..	6 37	..	..
—	Reedness Junction .. dep.	8 47	1134	....	2 13	4 58	7 31	8 1	....
19½	Goole 932, 939 .... arr.	9 0	1147	..	2 26	5 11	7 44	8 14	..

B Weds. and Sats. **E** or E Except Sats. **S** Sats. only.

North Lindsey Light Railway

Two weekday trains was the normal frequency - see the two example timetables below.

July 1913

SCUNTHORPE and WHITTON (**3rd class only**).—Great Central.

Miles.		Week Days only.						
		mrn	aft					
	Scunthorpe dep.	7 35	1 20	....	....	....	....	....
5	Winterton and Thealby	7 50	1 35	....	....	....	....	....
6	West Halton	7 53	1 38	....	....	....	....	....
8½	Winteringham	8 0	1 45	....	....	....	....	....
11	Whitton arr.	8 10	....	....	....	....	....	....

Miles.		Week Days only.						
		mrn	aft					
	Whitton dep.	8 15	....	....	....	....	....	....
2½	Winteringham	8 25	2 0	....	....	....	....	....
5	West Halton	8 32	2 7	....	....	....	....	....
6	Winterton and Thealby	8 35	2 10	....	....	....	....	....
11	Scunthorpe arr.	8 50	2 25	....	....	....	....	....

July 1921

SCUNTHORPE and WHITTON (**3rd class only**).—Great Central.

Miles.		Week Days only.					
		mrn	aft	Sats. only aft			
	Scunthorpe dep.	7 55	1 20	6 0	....	....	....
5	Winterton and Thealby	8 10	1 35	6 15	....	....	....
6	West Halton	8 13	1 38	6 18	....	....	....
8½	Winteringham	8 19	1 45	6 24	....	....	....
11	Whitton arr.	....	1 55		....	....	....

Miles.		Week Days only.					
		mrn	aft	Sats. only aft			
	Whitton dep.	....	2 0	....	....	....	....
2½	Winteringham	8 25	2 10	6 30	....	....	....
5	West Halton	8 32	2 17	6 37	....	....	....
6	Winterton and Thealby	8 35	2 20	6 40	....	....	....
11	Scunthorpe arr.	8 50	2 35	6 55	....	....	....

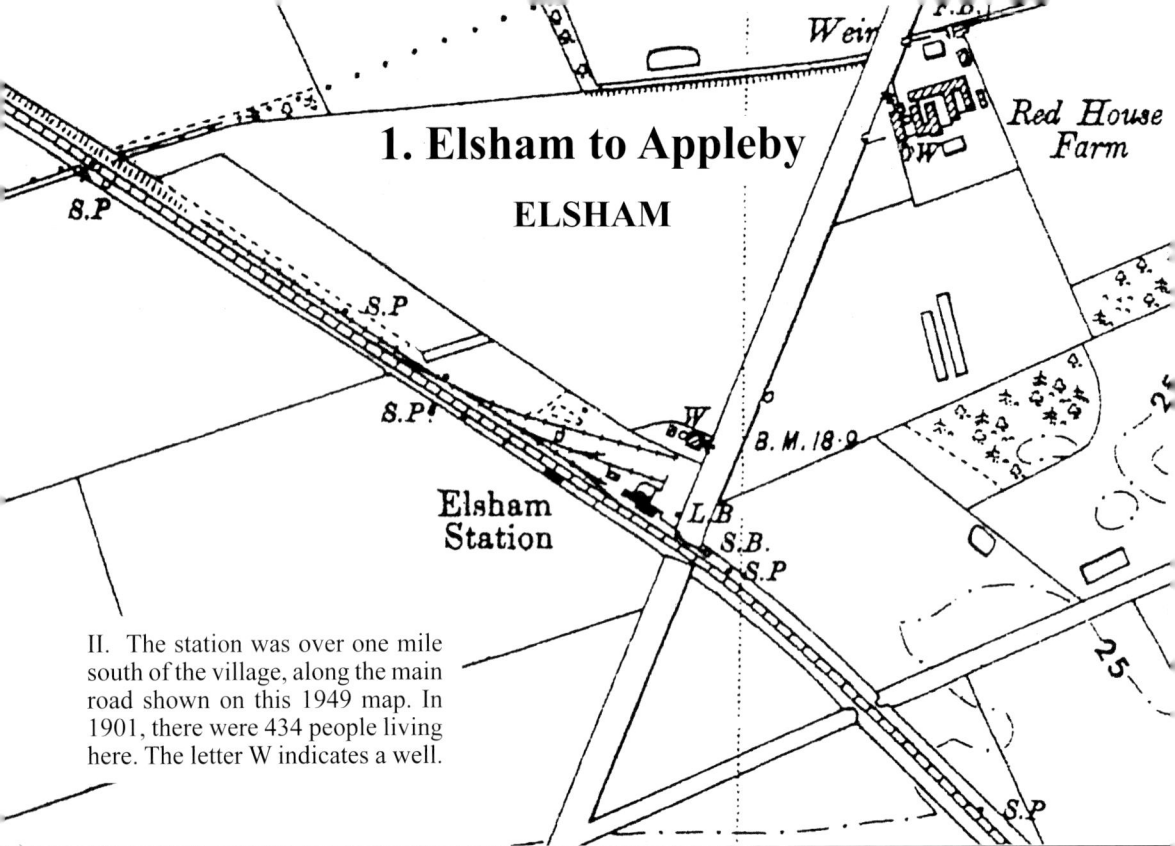

1. Elsham to Appleby

ELSHAM

Red House Farm

Elsham Station

II. The station was over one mile south of the village, along the main road shown on this 1949 map. In 1901, there were 434 people living here. The letter W indicates a well.

1.   Platforms were staggered, so that passengers would have to cross behind calling trains. There was usually a staff of one, with a station master, who shared duty with Appleby. This post ended in 1966 and the former on 29th September 1969. (P.Laming coll.)

2. A 1962 westward panorama includes the small goods yard, which was in use until 6th July 1964. There were two private sidings nearby, for lime traffic. Passenger service ceased here on 3rd October 1993. (R.Humm coll.)

3. A class 114 DMU in the short-lived South Yorkshire PTE brown and cream livery, comprising cars E53045 and E54004, recedes from Elsham with a train for Cleethorpes on 11th April 1984. The 22-lever signal box was listed in 1986 and closed on 30th December 2015. A panel had arrived on 3rd March 2003. (P.D.Shannon)

APPLEBY (LINCS.)

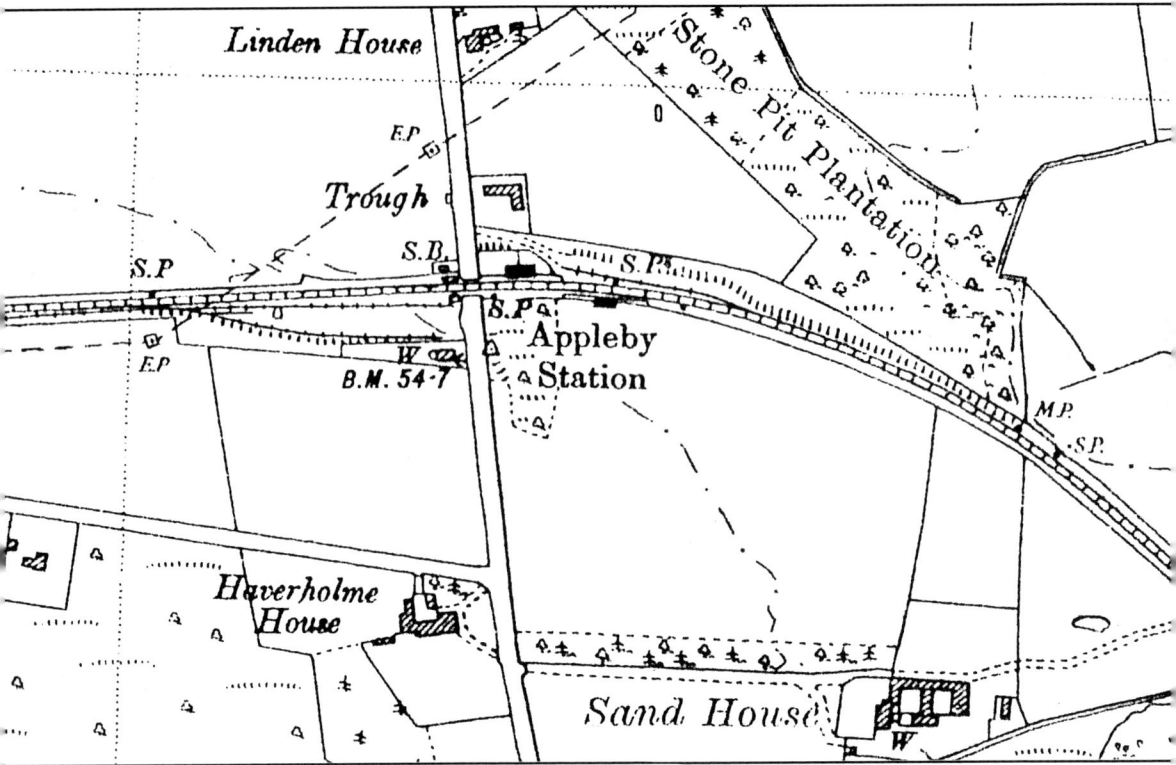

III. The year is 1949. The main road is Ermine Street, which was of Roman origin. E.P refers to Electricity Pylon. The goods yard had a 4 ton 14 cwt crane in the 1954 listing.

4.   This is the view east from the signal box in 1969 and it includes one of the three sidings. The running-in board has the suffix LINCS, which was added on 1st July 1923. The other station of that name was in Westmorland. There were 546 residents here in 1901. (R.Humm coll.)

5.   Nos 37094 and 37055 are passing the closed station with an Immingham Dock to Frodingham iron ore train on 29th July 1979. At least modern crossing lighting had arrived. (T.Heavyside)

6.   It would appear that the station building was demolished by 1983, when this photograph was taken. Goods traffic had ceased here on 6th July 1964 and passenger service was withdrawn on 5th June 1967. The structure on the right had once held the loading gauge. The 1886 signal box had 23 levers until replaced by a panel on 26th June 1972. (P.D.Shannon)

2. Scunthorpe to Doncaster

IV. Elsham station is noted at the right border, but the village is beyond it. Appleby and its station are shown on the B1207, further west. This 1946 edition has both Winterton and Whitton stations shown as closed, along with one other. Our entire route can be followed to the left border at ¼ in to 1 mile. Section 3 of this volume is from lower centre to upper centre.

2nd-SINGLE   SINGLE-2nd

Appleby (Lincs.) to

Appleby (Lincs.)   Appleby (Lincs.)
Doncaster   Doncaster

DONCASTER

via Althorpe

(E)   7/0   Fare   7/0   (E)

For conditions see over   For conditions see over

0243

L. N. E. R.   L. N. E. R.
DAY EXC'N   DAY EXC'N
Liberal Club   Liberal Club
Party Guaranteed   Party Guaranteed

BLACKPOOL   **APPLEBY (LINCS.)**

TO   TO

APPLEBY (LINCS.)   **BLACKPOOL**

Via Ashburys   Via Ashburys
17 SEPT. 1949   17 SEPT. 1949

THIRD   THIRD
For conditions   For conditions
see back   see back

0106

SCUNTHORPE

V. A four-times enlargement from the same era includes Althorpe and Scunthorpe stations. The latter is east of the A159 and the former is lower left. The lines to the numerous steel works are best studied with a lens. Gunness is lower left and its wharf, near its inn, was the point at which ironstone was unloaded from trains from Frodingham onto boats running north to other industrial areas. A long siding is evident here and on map VI. It ran to Gunness Wharf, which was still in use for commercial traffic in 2019.

7.   The original station, called Frodingham, opened with the line on 1st October 1866. This was around 1 mile east of the current site and became Frodingham & Scunthorpe in 1886. It was resited west of the former level crossing with Brigg Road, the A1029 in map V, on 2nd January 1888. Pictured is the third station, which opened on 11th March 1928 and is still in use. This early view includes LNER lettering. The town's population grew from 6750 in 1901 to 68,890 in 1961. (P.Laming coll.)

8.   The suffix '& Frodingham' was applied until 16th November 1963. The goods yard was in use from January 1929. This postcard features the new concrete footbridge and the 48-lever signal box, which was in use from 11th March 1928 until 31st March 1973. Nearest is a horse box. The bay had been used by Gunhouse banking engines resting between duties. (J.Alsop coll.)

9.   The motive power depot was known simply as Frodingham and was on the north side of the main line. Part of it is seen on 31st December 1931. By 1950, the allocation was 70. It dropped to 41 by 1965. The code was 36C and closure came in 1966. The yard is shown in picture 108. (R.Humm coll.)

2nd-SINGLE   SINGLE-2nd

1959   1959

Scunthorpe & Frodingham to

Scunthorpe &   Scunthorpe &
Frodingham   Frodingham
Althorpe   Althorpe

ALTHORPE

(E)   0/8   Fare   (E)

For conditions see over   For conditions see over

2nd-SINGLE   SINGLE-2nd

5626   5626

Scunthorpe & Frodingham to

Scunthorpe &   Scunthorpe &
Frodingham   Frodingham
Appleby (Lincs.)   Appleby (Lincs.)

APPLEBY (LINCS)

(E)   1/2   Fare   1/2   (E)

For conditions see over   For conditions see over

L. N. E. R.

FOR CONDITIONS SEE BACK. Available for
three days, including day of issue.

4033   4033

SCUNTHORPE & FRODINGHAM to

BARNBY DUN

Fare   S   2s 1½d.C
THIRD   / 2164 \   CLASS
          BARNBY DUN

2nd-SINGLE   SINGLE-2nd

20382   20382

Scunthorpe to

Scunthorpe   Scunthorpe
Crowle (Central)   Crowle (Central)

CROWLE (CENTRAL)

(E)   2/3   Fare   2/3   (E)

For conditions see over   For conditions see over

10.   Looking east from the footbridge on 3rd May 2012, we find that most of the sidings have been lifted. At least a good passenger service was on offer. Nearest is DMU no. 142096, which is about to start its return to Doncaster. Reversal was over the crossover beyond it. (P.Jones)

11.   Seen on 1st June 2019 is the new footbridge with lifts, which came into use in April of that year. Annual passenger usage rose from 376,870 in 2013-14 to 417,530 in 2017-18. In 2005, the station won 'The Loo of the Year' award, for its cleanliness. The single line on the right is included on diagram XXXI, near picture 99. (V.Mitchell)

WEST OF SCUNTHORPE

Gunhouse Junction

12.   Beware that spellings have varied in this district. This location is near the right border of the next map and is seen on 15th August 1967. The signal box was completed in about 1916, with 20 levers. East of here is Frodingham Viaduct, which is almost ½ mile in length and appears on map V. (J.Alsop coll.)

13.   We look from the steps of the same box as an excursion bound for Cleethorpes speeds east behind a class B1 4-6-0. In the up loop is class J11 0-6-0 no. 64308. The box had a new frame in 1953 and was closed on 29th October 1972. (R.Humm coll.)

Burringham Bridge

14.   Burringham is shown lower left on map V and was the name used for this bridge, close to Althorpe station. The two swing spans are to the right of the windmill. The structure was replaced by the one shown on the map and in pictures 15, 16 and 19. Gunhouse Wharf is shown as Ironstone Wharf on the next map. Gunness & Burringham station (1869-1916) was at the east end of the truncated line. (J.Alsop coll.)

Keadby Bridge

15.   The No. 1 caisson is suspended on jacks on 18th April 1913. The photo was taken from the old viaduct, seen in picture 14. Both names have been used by different authorities. The 1866 swing bridge had carried trains only. (R.Humm coll.)

16. Named the King George V Bridge, it was opened by him for railway and highway traffic on 21st May 1916. It crosses the Trent from Althorpe station to Gunness. Its steel structure was built by Sir William Arrol and Co Ltd and had a lifting span weighing 3600 tons. It was 165ft long and was operated by two 115hp electric motors. The other two spans were fixed. There were also two secondary spans on the east bank, on which the opening span rolled. (J.Alsop coll.)

2nd · SINGLE   SINGLE · 2nd

ALTHORPE TO

Althorpe   Althorpe
CROWLE (Cen.)   CROWLE (Cen.)

CROWLE (CENTRAL)

(E)   1/2   Fare   1/2   (E)
For conditions see over   For conditions see over

5961   5961

3rd · SINGLE   SINGLE · 3rd

ALTHORPE TO

Althorpe   Althorpe
SCUNTHORPE & F SCUNTHORPE & F

SCUNTHORPE & FRODING'M

(E) 0/7   Fare   0/7   (E)
For conditio   ver For conditions see over

3070   3070

BRITISH RLYS. (E) BRITISH RLYS. (E)
PRIVILEGE   PRIVILEGE
For conditions   For conditions
see back   see back
Available within one Available within one
week of date of issue week of date of issue
Althorpe   Althorpe
ALTHORPE to

SCUNTHORPE & F.
SCUNTHORPE &   SCUNTHORPE & F.

3rd. Class   3rd. Class

1931   1931

2nd · SINGLE

Althorpe To

THORNE
(SOUTH)

Fare 0/10
FOR CONDITIONS SEE OVER

3818 CHILD   CHILD 3818

ALTHORPE Keadby

Gunness

Methodist Chapel

St. Barnabas's Church

North Soak Drain

YORKSHIRE NAVIGATION STAINFORTH & KEADBY CANAL

South Soak Drain

South Yorkshire Hotel (P.H.)

B.M. 13.5

B.M. 13.1

Locks

Mud

High Water Ma

Double Ri

New Idle River

Pumping Engine

Windmill

RIVER TRENT

Pumping Sta.

B.M. 13.3

Hollywell Villa

B.M. 13.4

Friendship Terrace

Ironstone Wharf

Iro

School

Windmill

B.M. 19

B.M. 13.4

S.P.

Althorpe Station

S.P.

Mud

B.M. 17.2

L. N. E. R.
CHILD

5634   5634

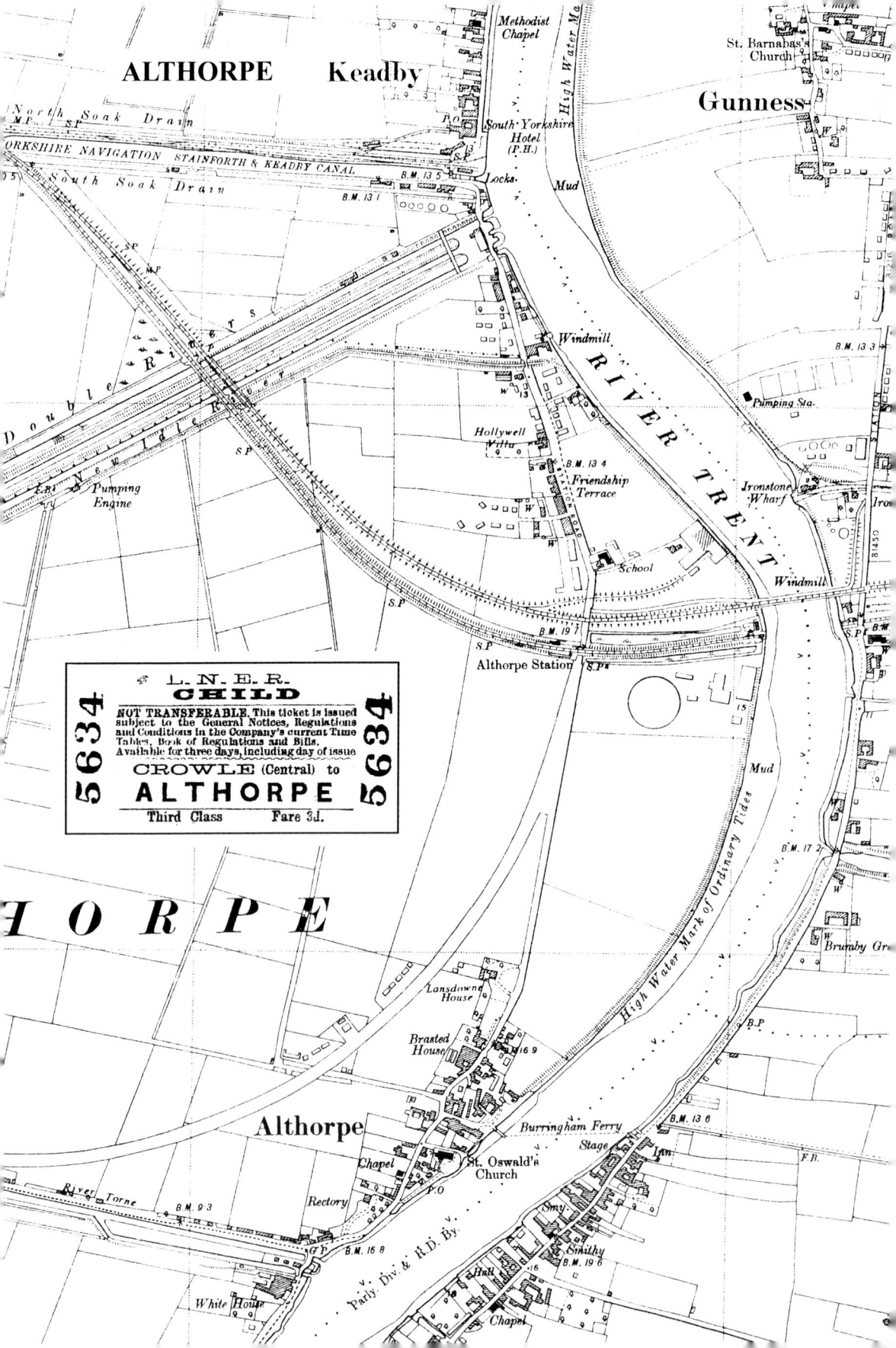

NOT TRANSFERABLE. This ticket is issued subject to the General Notices, Regulations and Conditions in the Company's current Time Tables, Book of Regulations and Bills. Available for three days, including day of issue

CROWLE (Central) to

ALTHORPE

Third Class   Fare 3d.

HORPE

High Water Mark of Ordinary Tides

Brumby Gr

Lansdowne House

Brasted House

B.M. 16.9

B.P.

Althorpe

Burringham Ferry

Stage

Inn

B.M. 13.6

F.B.

Chapel

St. Oswald's Church

P.O.

Smy

River Torne

B.M. 9.3

Rectory

Hall

Smithy

B.M. 19.6

G.P.

B.M. 16.8

Parly. Div. & R.D. By.

White House

Chapel

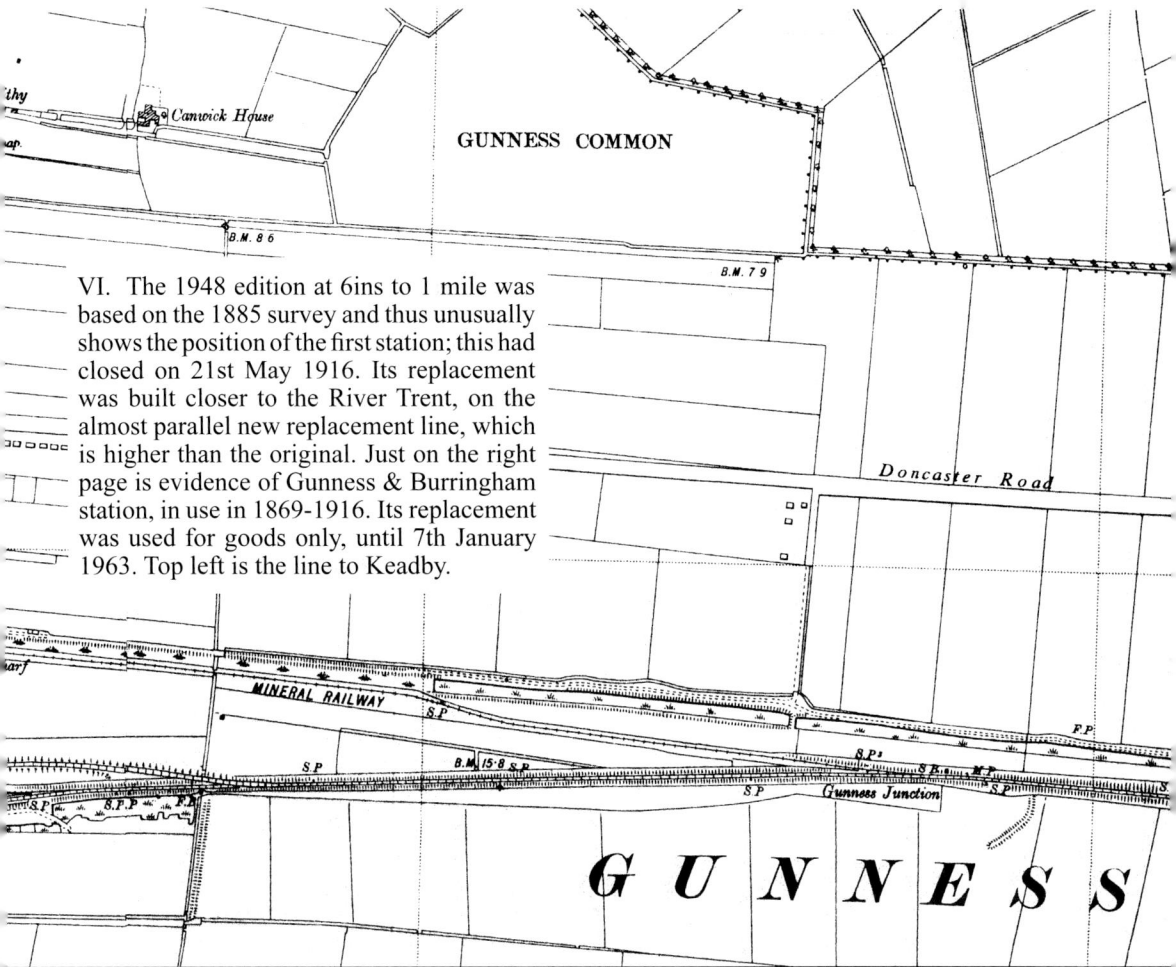

GUNNESS COMMON

Canwick House

B.M. 86

B.M. 79

VI. The 1948 edition at 6ins to 1 mile was based on the 1885 survey and thus unusually shows the position of the first station; this had closed on 21st May 1916. Its replacement was built closer to the River Trent, on the almost parallel new replacement line, which is higher than the original. Just on the right page is evidence of Gunness & Burringham station, in use in 1869-1916. Its replacement was used for goods only, until 7th January 1963. Top left is the line to Keadby.

Doncaster Road

MINERAL RAILWAY

SP

B.M. 15·8 SP

SP

SP

Gunness Junction

SP

FP

FP

SP.P

SP

SP

SP

SP

SP

G U N N E S S

17. This is the platform shown on the map. The running-in board says 'Keadby and Althorpe'; all a bit confusing! The signal box had a 13-lever frame and was in use from 1889 to 21st May 1916. (P.Laming coll.)

18. Here is another view from about 1910. It is clear that the first station was on a sharp curve. The village housed 539 in 1901. (J.Alsop coll.)

↓ 19. On 3rd March 1984 the 10.45 Manchester Piccadilly-Cleethorpes train runs through the new station, trailed by a DMU power car of class 124. This was one vehicle of eight six-car sets built at Swindon in 1960-61 for Trans-Pennine services. After 1977, they were supplemented by class 123s from the Western Region, and both types were withdrawn later in 1984. Note the down side waiting shelter of a modern design. The shadow of the old building is on the right. The A18 runs parallel on the left-hand side and both road and railway cross the River Trent. A freighter is tied up at Gunness Wharf. The bridge was controlled from a wooden signal cabin, mounted by the northeast side of the lifting (east) span. It was fitted out with a 28-lever frame of British Pneumatic Railway Signal Company design. The bridge had not been lifted since 1956. It was widened and the headroom increased in 1960, but the bascule was fixed in position. The bascule is the hinged portion of the bridge. At the same time, the signal cabin was removed from the bridge structure. (A.C.Hartless)

20. Keadby Swing Bridge appears on the last map, top left. Left is the structure which spans the canal when a train is due and is seen on 18th October 2006. (Colour-Rail.com)

21. The curved fence bars near no. 66781 help locate the picture position. It was taken on 6th December 2018, soon after a new bridge span had arrived. The 1926 Keadby Canal Junction signal box had 36 levers at its optimum. They were reduced to 10 in about 1972. (J.Whitehouse)

KEADBY

22. We have no views of the station, as it only served passengers from September 1859 to 2nd November 1874. However, goods continued until 30th April 1971. On 1st October 1866, it was renamed 'Keadby for Amcotts & Burringham'. The Keadby Canal wharfage is on the left and the northern extension of the Ironstone Wharf is on the right. Boat loading was by shovel and gravity. (J.Alsop coll.)

23. An engine shed was maintained here until a new one at Frodingham came into use in 1932. The picture is from May 1932 and the shed is shown on map VI. The population was 720 in 1901. (J.Alsop coll.)

24.   Seen at Keadby Jetty on 21st April 1963 is a two-car class 114 DMU (nos E56003 and E50003) with the Railway Enthusiasts Club 'North Lindseyman Railtour'. The power station was gas-fired from January 1996. (D.Lawrence/Photos from the Fifties)

25.   Keadby Power Works signal box opened in 1951 with 20 levers and was worked until March 1970. It is seen on 29th May 1965, with no. 90156, an ex-WD 2-8-0 classified 8F. Keadby Power Station was built on the site of a former coal-fired power station, which opened on 1st April 1952, but closed in 1984. (R.Humm coll.)

CROWLE CENTRAL

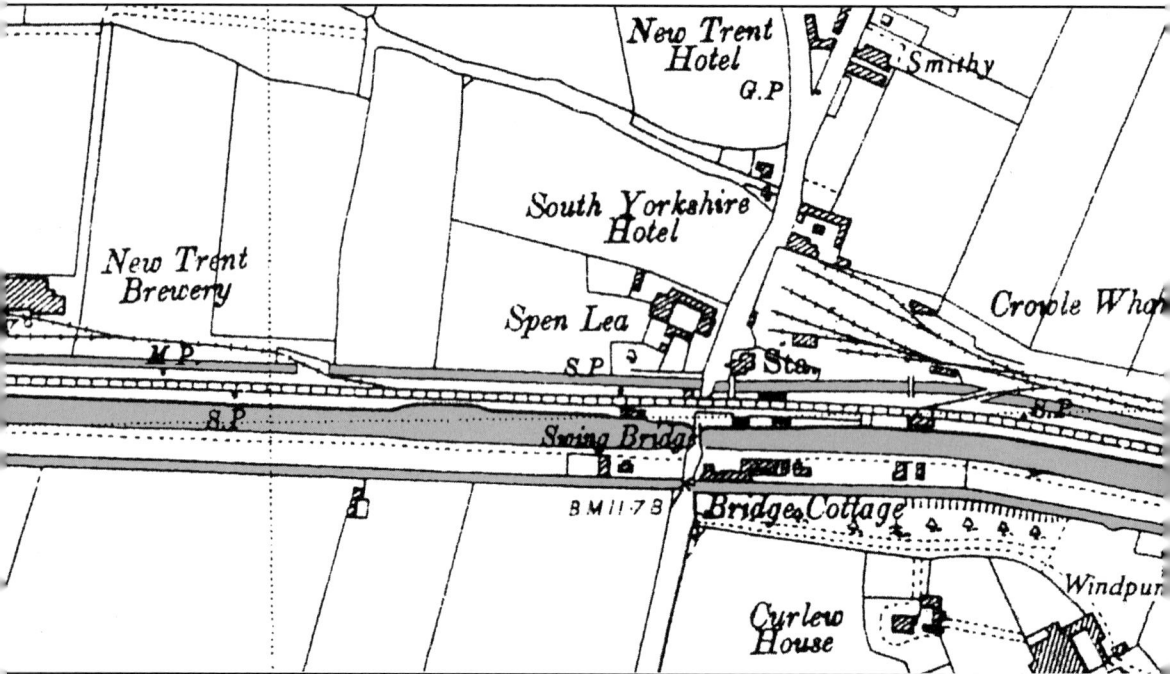

VII. There are three water courses across this 1949 map, scaled at 6ins to 1 mile. Crowle Wharf is adjacent to the first one, which passes under the connection to the goods yard. The widest one carries the words 'Swing Bridge' and the third is above 'Bridge Cottage'. The station opened early, on 13th September 1859.

26. A view eastwards from about 1905 shows the connection beyond the crossover dropping steeply to the goods yard and wharf. The large chimney is above the water pump, which supplied the tank beyond it. The four chimney pots served staff dwellings. (J.Alsop coll.)

27.   The tank just seen would have supplied this water column, as well as the one just north of it. In the distance is New Trent Brewery, which had a private siding. There was also one for a brickworks listed in 1938. A 30cwt crane was on offer. Public goods traffic ceased on 5th April 1965. (J.Alsop coll.)

28.   The full name of the canal is top left on map VI and the short swing bridge is on map VII. The level crossing gates are between it and the signal box. It had 25 levers from about 1886 to 1955. Crowle housed 2769 in 1901 and 3010 in 1961. (P.Laming coll.)

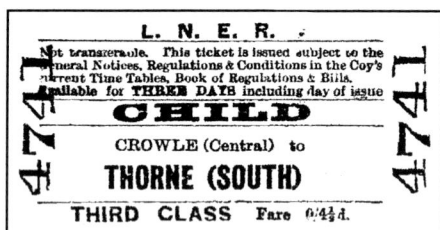

L. N. E. R.
Not transferable. This ticket is issued subject to the
General Notices, Regulations & Conditions in the Coy's
current Time Tables, Book of Regulations & Bills.
Available for THREE DAYS including day of issue.
CHILD
CROWLE (Central) to
THORNE (SOUTH)
THIRD CLASS   Fare 0/4½d.
4741   4741

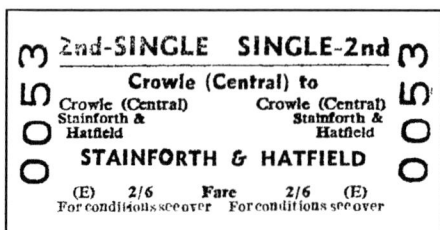

0053   2nd-SINGLE   SINGLE-2nd   0053
Crowle (Central) to
Crowle (Central)   Crowle (Central)
Stainforth &   Stainforth &
Hatfield   Hatfield
STAINFORTH & HATFIELD
(E)   2/6   Fare   2/6   (E)
For conditions see over   For conditions see over

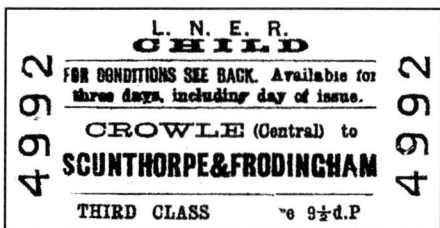

L. N. E. R.
CHILD
FOR CONDITIONS SEE BACK. Available for
three days, including day of issue.
CROWLE (Central) to
SCUNTHORPE&FRODINGHAM
THIRD CLASS   ·e 9½d.P
4992   4992

29. The suffix CENTRAL was in use from 1st July 1923 until 20th February 1969 and is seen in 1959, on the running-in board. All platform weather protection had become life expired. In the distance is the embankment, which carried the Haxey-Reedness Junction line. The southern bridge abutment could still be found in 2019. (Stations UK)

➚ 30. No. 40086 heads west with a Speedlink train from Immingham Docks on 13th April 1983. The road on the left used to continue with a level crossing over the railway and a swing bridge over the Stainforth & Keadby Canal; both were replaced in 1972 by a high-level bridge, on which the photographer is standing. The 1955 signal box had 45 levers and closed on 15th October 1972. (P.D.Shannon)

➙ 31. This eastward vista was recorded from beyond the site of the box on 7th November 2018 and it includes a ground-level crossing for passengers. Units present are nos 185111 and 142093. The spacious relay room is on the right. (A.J.Booth)

GODKNOW BRIDGE

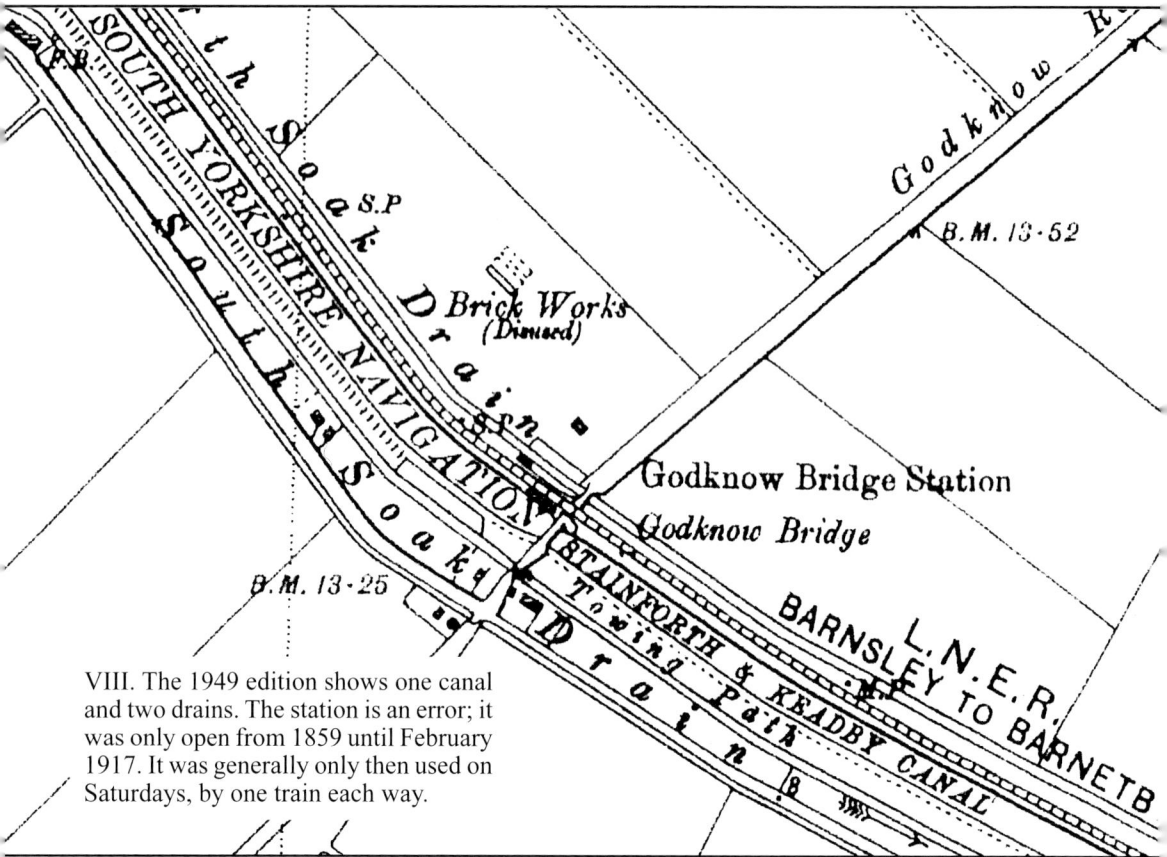

VIII. The 1949 edition shows one canal and two drains. The station is an error; it was only open from 1859 until February 1917. It was generally only then used on Saturdays, by one train each way.

32.   This postcard was undated, but records state that the signal box opened with 10 levers in 1886. They were replaced by a panel in 1981. A replica of the original box came into use on 15th August 2000. It was still staffed in 2019. The location is about one mile southwest of the centre of Crowle. (J.Alsop coll.)

*Medge Hall
Peat Works*

Medge *Hall*

G.C.R.

BARNSLEY TO BAR

STAINFORTH & Mc KEADBY

Station

Crook o' Moor Bridge
(Swing)

UTH YORKSHIRE NAVIGATION

Path

Drain

*Crook o' Moor
Farm*

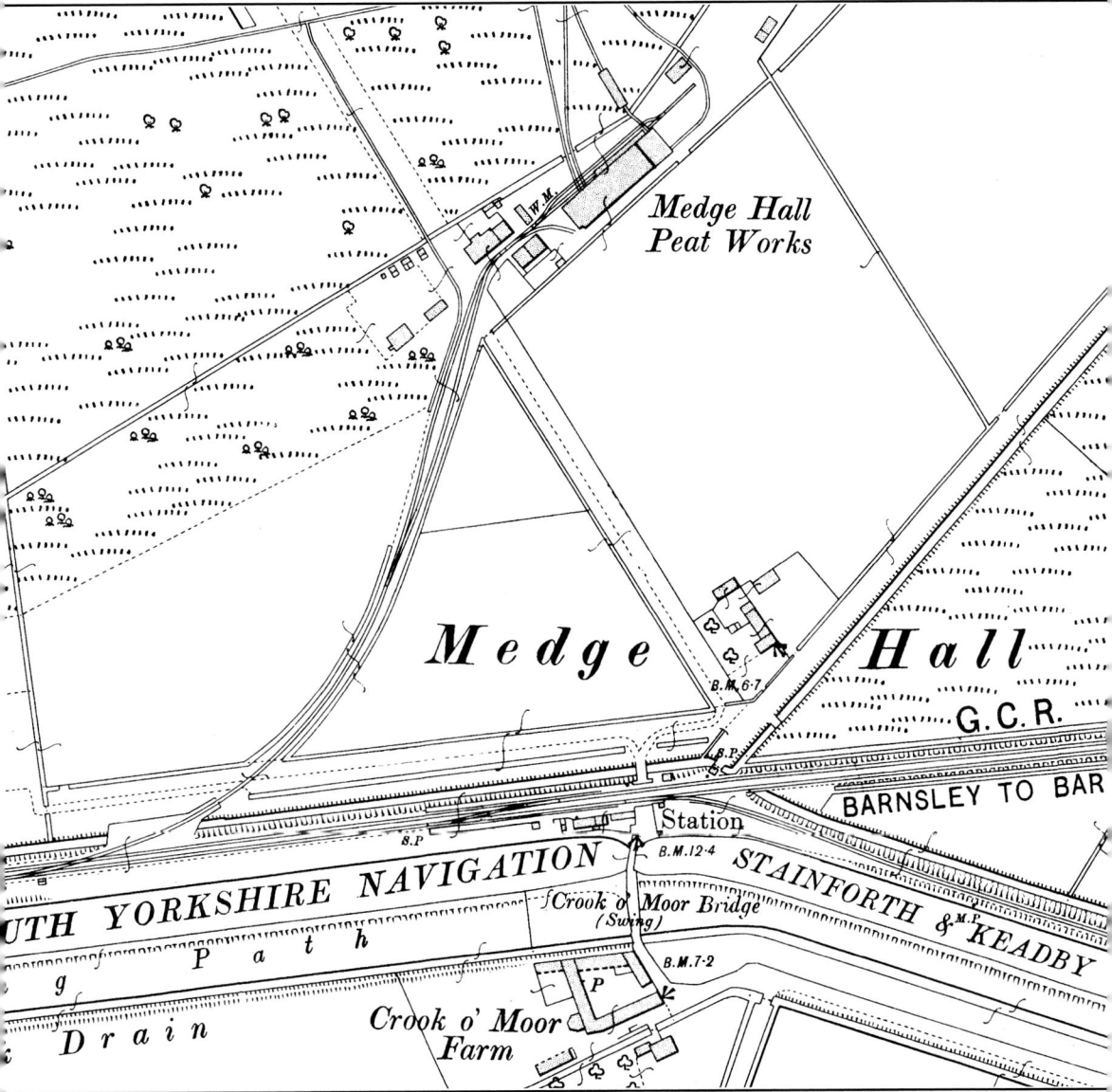

IX. The 1906 issue at 25ins to 1 mile includes a long siding south of the main line and a private siding for peat north of it. The lines north from the works had portable rails and ran for about two miles. Horse power was used for many years.

GREAT CENTRAL RAILWAY.
Issued subject to the Regulations and Conditions in the Company's Time Tables, Books, Bills, & Notices.
ON DATE OF ISSUE ONLY.
MEDGE HALL
TO
THORNE
THIRD CLASS
FARE 3½d

MR·10·0

1408

L N E R
CHILD
Not Transferable. This ticket is issued subject to the General Notices, Regulations, Conditions in the Co's current time tables. Available on day of issue only.
MEDGE HALL to
Via **CROWLE**
THIRD CLASS   Fare 4

050   050

33. A Bradford to Cleethorpes excursion speeds east on 19th July 1958 behind no. 61142, a class B1 4-6-0 ex-LNER. The station closed to passengers on 12th September 1960 and to goods on 4th May 1964. The building backs onto the wide canal. (R.Humm coll.)

34. No. 144001 is running from Scunthorpe to Lincoln on 21st December 2016. The original 1886 signal box had 16 levers at the most by the 1960s, but was down to seven from May 1972. A replica box was still staffed in 2019. (J.Whitehouse)

Mauds Bridge

This rural station was about a mile west of Medge Hall station, which is shown on map IV. There was a 13-lever signal box nearby from 1886 to 1972. The station was open from 10th September 1859 to 1st October 1866 only.

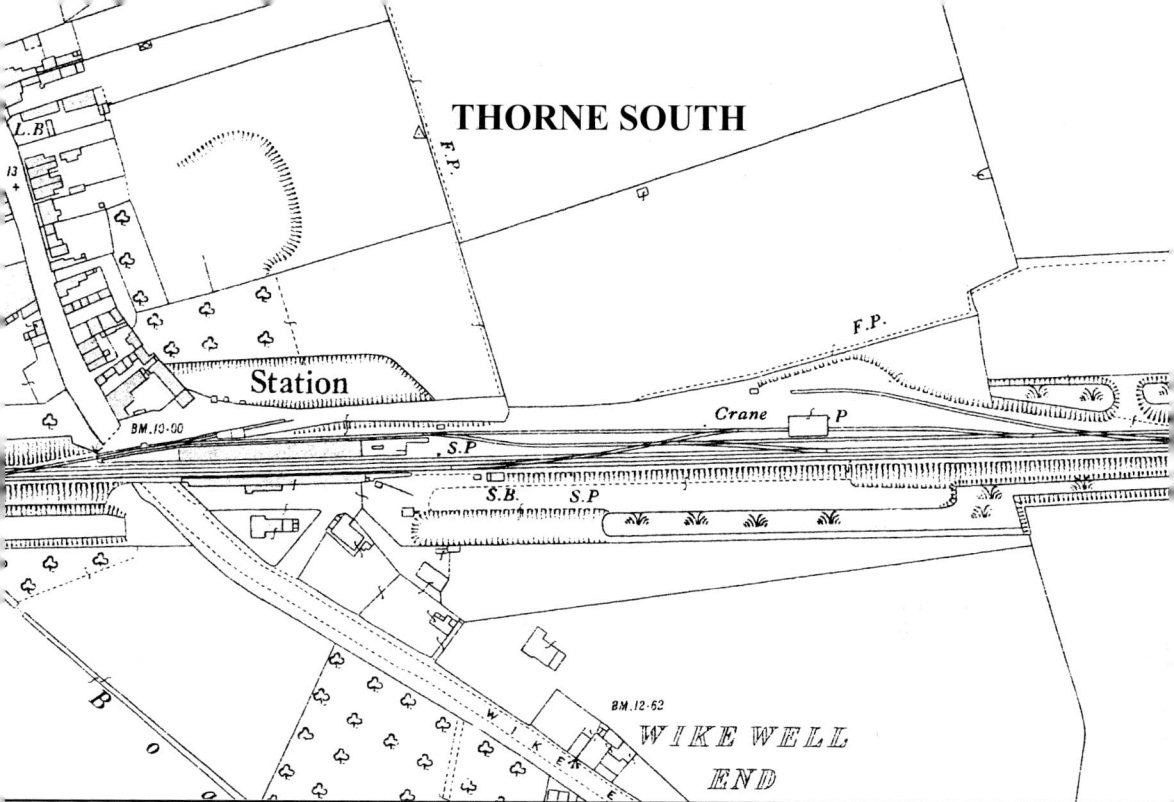

THORNE SOUTH

Station

X. The 1932 edition is at 20ins to 1 mile. Thorne had 3818 residents in the 1901 census. In 1938 the crane was of 5-ton capacity. The first station was called THORNE LOCK and had been near Thorne, opening in 1856. The second had been even closer and was open in 1859-66, without a suffix. The third station was on the direct line and opened in 1866. The word SOUTH was added on 1st July 1923.

35. Included are all three platforms, plus the steel components of the bridge over the main road. Major alterations came in the mid-1970s, when the left platform was eliminated, all the roofing was removed and the subway was filled in. Little trace remains. (J.Alsop coll.)

36. The crane is beyond the loading gauge in this view of WD 2-8-0 no. 90315 on 29th May 1965. The yard closed on 5th April of that year. The 1886 signal box had 20 levers initially and was named SOUTH from 1917. (R.Humm coll.)

37. The population rose to 15,280 by 1961 and annual passenger figures were over 87,000 by 2015. No. 66564 approaches on 4th July 2008, as a class 142 DMU leaves. A fully accessible ramped footbridge now links the two platforms - this was opened in July 2013 to replace this old barrow crossing, which had been the scene of several 'near misses', prior to a passenger being injured by a passing train whilst trying to cross the line in January 2013. (A.J.Booth)

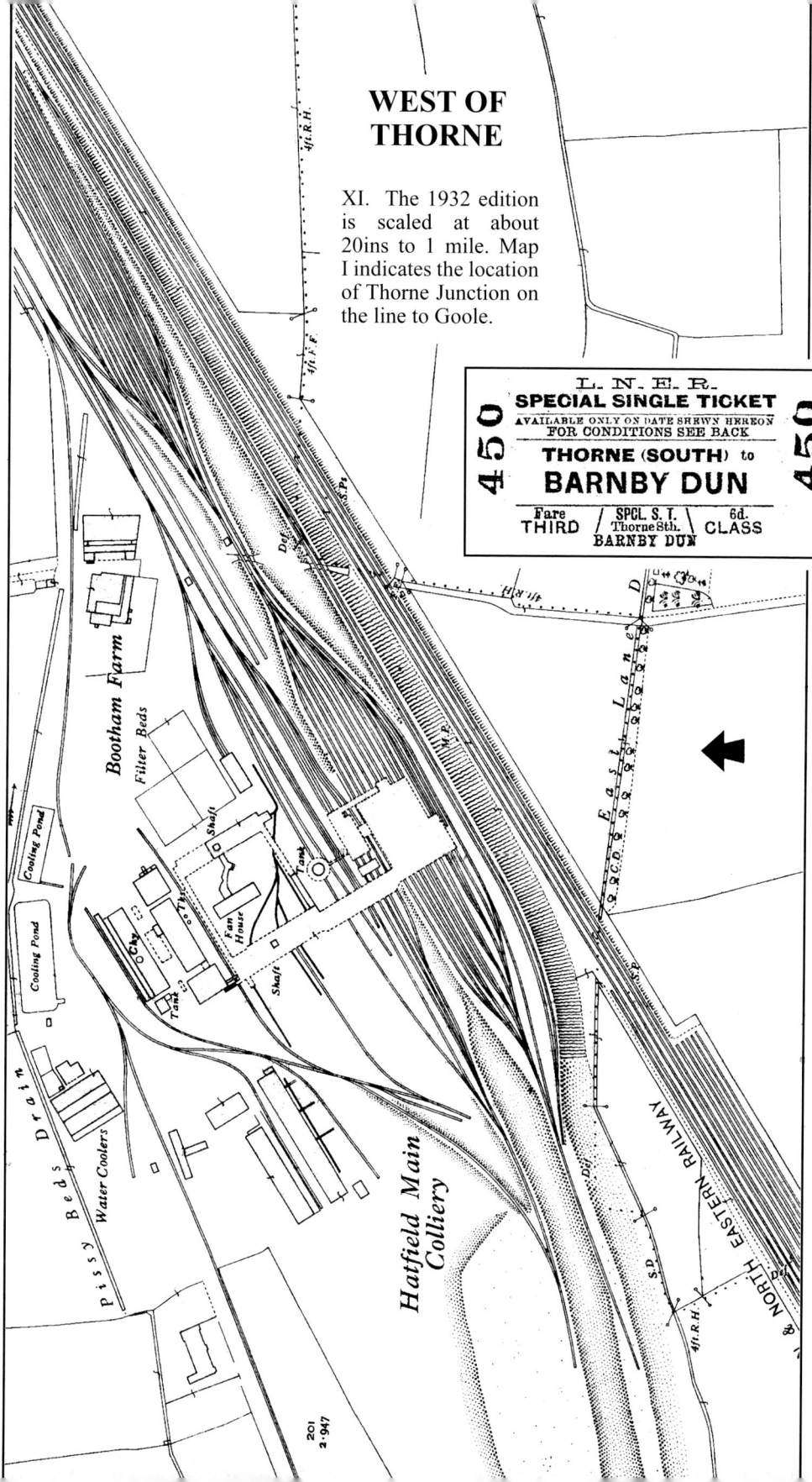

WEST OF THORNE

XI. The 1932 edition is scaled at about 20ins to 1 mile. Map I indicates the location of Thorne Junction on the line to Goole.

L. N. E. R.
SPECIAL SINGLE TICKET
AVAILABLE ONLY ON DATE SHEWN HEREON
FOR CONDITIONS SEE BACK
THORNE (SOUTH) to
BARNBY DUN

450   450

Fare	SPCL S.T.	6d.
THIRD	Thorne Sth.	CLASS
	BARNBY DUN	

Bootham Farm

Filter Beds

Cooling Pond

Cooling Pond

Pissy Beds Drain

Water Coolers

Hatfield Main Colliery

Fan House

Shaft

Shaft

Chy.

Tank

East Lane

NORTH EASTERN RAILWAY

Hatfield Main Colliery

38. No. 47291 enters Stainforth & Hatfield station on 5th June 1980 with a merry-go-round coal train that has just passed through the rapid loader in the background. Track remodelling and resignalling was under way and the semaphores would all be gone by 29th June 1980, when control of the area passed to Doncaster power signal box. By 2019 only winding towers stood in parts.(P.D.Shannon)

39. No. 66190 is exercising its strength while loading a train on 1st April 2003. The colliery had raised its first coal in 1916, when much hand labour was used. There had been a merger in 1967-78 and a takeover in 2001, but it wound its last coal in 2004. However, there was a fresh production era in 2007-14, but a major landslip of a rain-soaked spoil heap in February 2013 closed the main line until July of that year. Formal pit closure was on 30th June 2015. (A.J.Booth)

HATFIELD & STAINFORTH

LONDON & NORTH EASTERN RAILWAY

S.D.

4ft.R.H.

D

4ft.R.H.

Stainforth *Carrs*

Carr House

Stainforth *Carrs*

S.P.

S.P.

S.P.

S.A.

S.Ps.

AVENUE

St. George's Villas

ROAD

RNE TERRACE

Stainforth & Hatfield Station

ing George Hotel (P.H.)

The Laurels

S.B.

S.Ps.

4ft.F.F.

Goods Shed

B.M.39.41

4ft.R.H.

D

s

k

r

a

P

XII. The 1932 survey is scaled at 20ins to 1 mile and shows the southern part of Stainforth. The centre of Hatfield is over one mile to the southeast. The quadruple track starts in the north at Thorne Junction and continues to Kirk Sandall. The station names shown on the map were reversed on 28th September 1992.

40. A northward panorama from the road bridge in about 1920 has the outline of the new colliery in the left background. Local freight traffic was segregated - coal right and goods left, a widespread practice in urban areas. Also on the right is a small cattle dock. (J.Alsop coll.)

41. This view south is from 1971 and includes the goods shed and the roofless area signed GENTLEMEN. Hatfield had housed 1606 in 1901, while Stainforth had just 735. (R.Humm coll.)

42. The main station building and the entrance are on the right in this 1970s presentation, looking northwards. The footbridge had to be used to reach the three platforms on the left. The other end of Stainforth Junction signal box is seen in the next picture. (R.Humm coll.)

GREAT CENTRAL RAILWAY.
Issued subject to the Regulations and Conditions of the Company's TimeTables, Books, Bills & Notices
ON DATE OF ISSUE ONLY.
STAINFORTH&Hatfield
TO
DONCASTER
THIRD CLASS
FARE 7d

L.N.E.R.
NOT TRANSFERABLE
Issued subject to theRegulations and Conditions in the Company's Time Tables, Books,Bills&Notices
ON DATE OF ISSUE ONLY
STAINFORTH&Hatfield
TO
LEEDS(C)
via Doncaster
THIRD CLASS   Fare 4s.5d.
Stainforth   Stainforth
LeedsC   LeedsC

L.N.E.R.
Not Transferable. This ticket is issued subject to the General Notices,Regulations&Conditions in the Coy's current time tables. Available on day of issue only
STAINFORTH&HATFIELD TO
SHEFFIELD (Vic.)
Fare   S.   3s2d
THIRD   Stainf'th&H   CLASS
          SheffieldVc

M. S. & L. R.
Issued subject to the printed conditions and regulations of the Company
Available on date of issue only
STAINFORTH
TO
WATH
THIRD CLASS
Stainforth   Stainforth
Wath   Wath
FARE 1/4

43. Track staff make observations sometime in 1977. The signal box had opened on 1st December 1916 with a 76-lever frame. This was extended to 95 on 3rd March 1940, when wartime traffic had become very demanding. It was reduced to 77 when supplemented by a panel on 5th June 1972. (Colour-Rail.com)

44. No. 1 platform is hidden by bushes and No. 2 has a black fence on its far side in this view from 10th October 2015. Both are served by steps and step-free ramps. The same applies at the entrance on the right. Nos 20301 and 20302 are working a railhead treatment train. Hatfield Main Colliery is in the background. Passengers had a 30-minute interval weekday service here generally, as half the trains served Hull. (A.J.Booth)

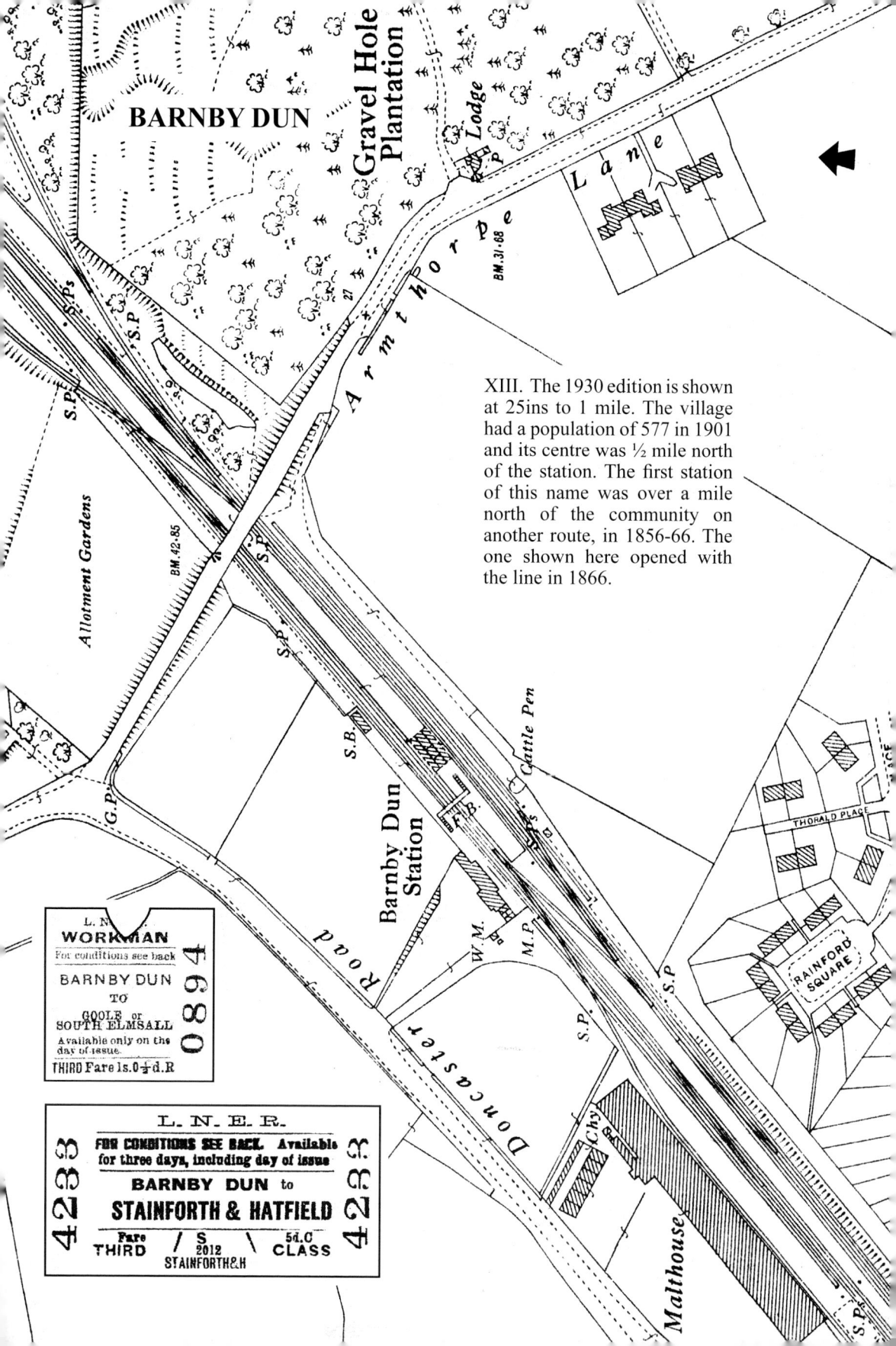

BARNBY DUN

Gravel Hole Plantation

Lodge

Armthorpe Lane

BM.31·68

Allotment Gardens

BM.42·85

S.B.

Barnby Dun Station

Cattle Pen

F.B.

Doncaster Road

W.M.

M.P.

THORALD PLACE

RAINFORD SQUARE

Malthouse

XIII. The 1930 edition is shown at 25ins to 1 mile. The village had a population of 577 in 1901 and its centre was ½ mile north of the station. The first station of this name was over a mile north of the community on another route, in 1856-66. The one shown here opened with the line in 1866.

L. N. E. R.

WORKMAN

For conditions see back

BARNBY DUN
TO
GOOLE or
SOUTH ELMSALL

Available only on the day of issue.

THIRD Fare 1s.0½d.R

0894

L. N. E. R.

FOR CONDITIONS SEE BACK. Available for three days, including day of issue

BARNBY DUN to
STAINFORTH & HATFIELD

Fare
THIRD / S \ 5d.C
2012   CLASS
STAINFORTH&H

4233

45.   This and the next picture were taken from the same bridge, but the main common feature is the white cattle dock. This shows the site before track quadrupling began in 1913. The signal box had 15 levers and was worked from about 1882 until 30th June 1916, when the box below opened. (J.Alsop coll.)

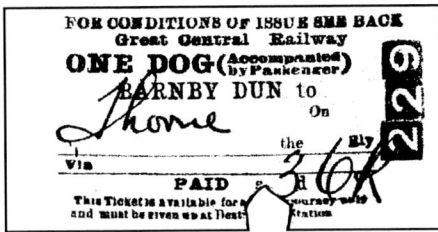

FOR CONDITIONS OF ISSUE SEE BACK
Great Central Railway
ONE DOG (Accompanied by Passenger)
BARNBY DUN to
On
the   Rly
PAID
Via
This Ticket is available for a journey and must be given up at Next Station

2229

7189

L. N. E. R.
CHILD
FOR CONDITIONS SEE BACK. Available for three days, including day of issue.
BARNBY DUN to
DONCASTER CENTRAL
Third Class   Fare 4½d.C

7189

46.   The new box had 72 levers and was in use until 10th December 1972. The goods yard had one long siding and closed on 5th April 1965. The LBSC round ended wagon (lower left) is a long way from home! Passenger service continued until 4th September 1967. (J.Alsop coll.)

47.   No. D6735 roars through with a down mineral train on 5th June 1965 and is about to run over the barrow crossing. The camera is on the footbridge. The station building was demolished in July 2008. (R.Humm coll.)

48.   GB Railfreight no. 66748 backs into the glassworks at Barnby Dun after working the 08.20 sand train from Middleton Towers-Barnby Dun on 29th September 2017. The train comprises two-axle PAA covered hopper wagons, which were built for British Industrial Sand in 1981-82; they would soon be replaced by modern bogie vehicles. (P.D.Shannon)

KIRK SANDALL

49. The first station, called Sandall, was on the temporary route from 1857 to 1859, the line closing in 1866. This station opened on 15th March 1991 to serve a growing suburb of Doncaster. It is 9th January 2017 and DMU no. 158795 passes with the 12.52 Doncaster-Hull. As at Hatfield & Stainforth, the fast lines are flanked by the slow ones, but here the solution to providing a passenger station was an island platform reached by a ramp from a nearby road. Annual usage soon exceeded 0.1m. (A.C.Hartless)

50. Here the photographer was lucky with a visit from a Rail Measurements Train. This had left Derby at breakfast time and reached here by way of Trent, Pye Bridge, Mansfield, Worksop, Retford (reverse), Shireoaks and Maltby. It has joined our route at Kirk Sandall Junction, which was half a mile behind the photographer. The four-coach train was topped and tailed by nos 37610 and 37602, and we see the rearward loco as the train creeps along the up slow line. The train spent the rest of a long day in the West Riding. (A.C.Hartless)

SOUTH OF KIRK SANDALL

51.   Kirk Sandall Junction is included on the left of map IV and is at the north end of an effective 'Doncaster Bypass'. It was opened in 1909 by the South Yorkshire Joint Railway and is on the right of this northward view from 1963. At work is no. 63914, a 2-8-0 of class O4. (Colour-Rail.com)

52.   No. 158784 is running south on 21st November 2015, having just reached the end of the quadruple track. The start of the 'South Yorkshire' single line is on the right. (A.J.Booth)

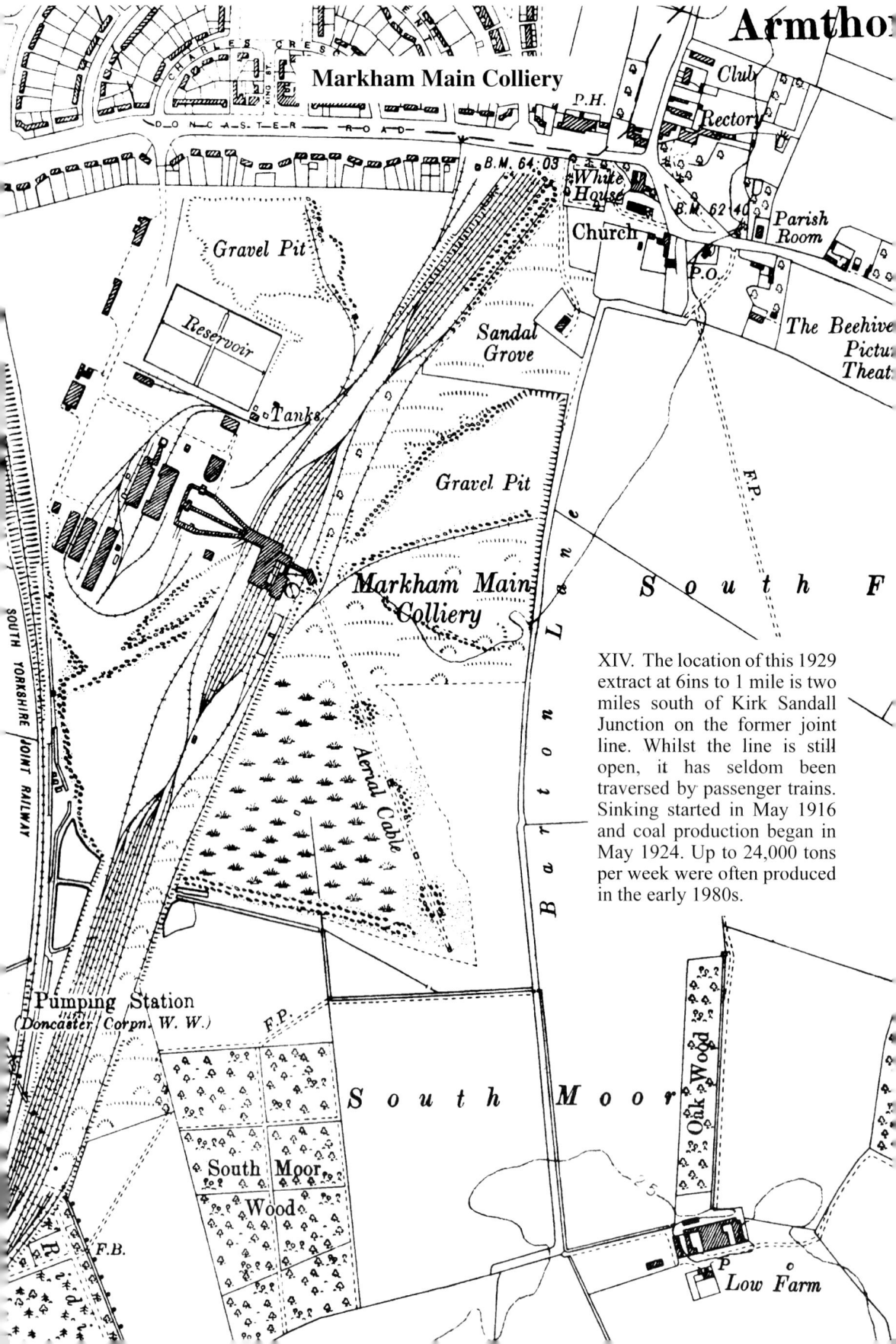

Armthor

Markham Main Colliery

CHARLES CRES

KINK TER

Club

Rectory

DONCASTER ROAD

P.H.

B.M. 64.03

White House

B.M. 62.40

Parish Room

Church

The Beehive Picture Theat

P.O.

Gravel Pit

Reservoir

Sandal Grove

Tanks

Gravel Pit

Markham Main Colliery

SOUTH TORKSHIRE JOINT RAILWAY

Aerial Cable

Barton Lane

S o u t h   F

XIV. The location of this 1929 extract at 6ins to 1 mile is two miles south of Kirk Sandall Junction on the former joint line. Whilst the line is still open, it has seldom been traversed by passenger trains. Sinking started in May 1916 and coal production began in May 1924. Up to 24,000 tons per week were often produced in the early 1980s.

Pumping Station (Doncaster Corpn. W.W.)

F.P.

F.P.

S o u t h   M o o r

Oak Wood

South Moor Wood

F.B.

P

Low Farm

53. Hunslet 0-6-0ST no. 3782 of 1953 was photographed on 29th March 1974, at the pit. This closed in 1996, when it had 50 million tonnes of coal reserves, enough for about 50 years. The site is now a housing estate, next to Sandall Beat Wood and there is no trace visible from a passing train. (T.Heavyside)

54. Seen on 4th August 1975 is *Robert*. It is an 0-4-0 diesel hydraulic machine produced by the Hunslet Engine Company as no. 7405 in 1974. (A.J.Booth)

NORTH OF DONCASTER

55. Marshgate Goods signal box was close to the River Don, which is on the next map. It opened in about 1873 with 18 levers. It had a new 30-lever frame in 1939 and is seen in 1974. Closure came on 8th July 1979. (N.D.Mundy)

56. This northward panorama is from 19th March 1939 and features Marshgate Junction box (left) and Marshgate Goods Yard (right). The complex bridges span the river. Our route curves right at the junction. The box opened in 1873 and closed on 8th July 1979. (Milepost 92½)

DONCASTER

XV. The 1904 edition at 6ins to 1 mile has our route upper border, centre. The northern avoiding lines from Bentley Junction and its three flyovers are beyond that border. Upper left is the almost straight line to York and curving left from it is the route to Wakefield. The River Don is upper left and winding below it is the River Cheswold. The largest black area represents the station. The many buildings to the left of it represent 'The Plant', which grew steadily as the line's locomotive and rolling stock manufactory. It is still busy.

57. The first station of 1848 was replaced by this fine structure, which was opened on 16th September 1850. This is its east elevation in about the 1890s. The down platform had become an island in the mid-1870s. (P.Laming coll.)

58. The suffix CENTRAL was in use in 1923-51. The footbridge was exclusively for workers in The Plant and is shown thus on the map. Platform 8 was the western one; four of them were bays. This 1948 view has a northbound train, but no details. (Stations UK)

59. It is 11th March 1982 and this northward view is included to emphasise that mail traffic was still substantial and that much was carried on passenger trains. F refers to the coach position on an InterCity 125 train and not the platform. (D.A.Thompson)

60. The date is 23rd June 1999 and Sprinter no. 156486 calls at platform 8, the down passenger loop, with the 10.43 Sheffield-Hull. The ends of bay platforms 6 and 7 are on the left, separated by a siding that was probably an engine release road in earlier times. To the right of the DMU are up and down goods lines, with reception sidings for The Plant loco and carriage works beyond. (A.C.Hartless)

61. No. 58002 is running south at 16.58 on 12th May 1999, with a long train of Merry-Go-Round hoppers. Electrification of the route from Peterborough and on to Leeds had taken place on 11th May 1987. The usual 25kV AC was used, but it did not help class 58s. (P.G.Barnes)

For other views, including The Plant, see our *Lincoln to Doncaster,*
Mansfield to Doncaster **and** *Newark to Doncaster* **volumes.**
Doncaster Trolleybuses **tells a local story.**

62. It is 1st June 2019 and a class 185 is entering platform 8, forming the late-running 11.37 service to Cleethorpes. In the background are stored class 331 units waiting introduction to traffic. (V.Mitchell)

3. Axholme Joint Railway

HAXEY JUNCTION

Haxey to Fockerby

1760 7.691 *Warping Drain*

L. & Y. & N.E.R.
AXHOLME JOINT RAILWAY

XVI. This 1921 edition is at 25ins to 1 mile and has our route on the right. The single line in the top left corner was used for freight only to Misson, on the Tickhill Light Railway and just in 1912-14. The second from Misson south to Bawtry carried goods until 1965 and was operated by the GNR until 1923. Our journey starts at the station on the right. The entire route can be found on map IV and more details are included in our *Newark to Doncaster* album, in pictures 70-73.

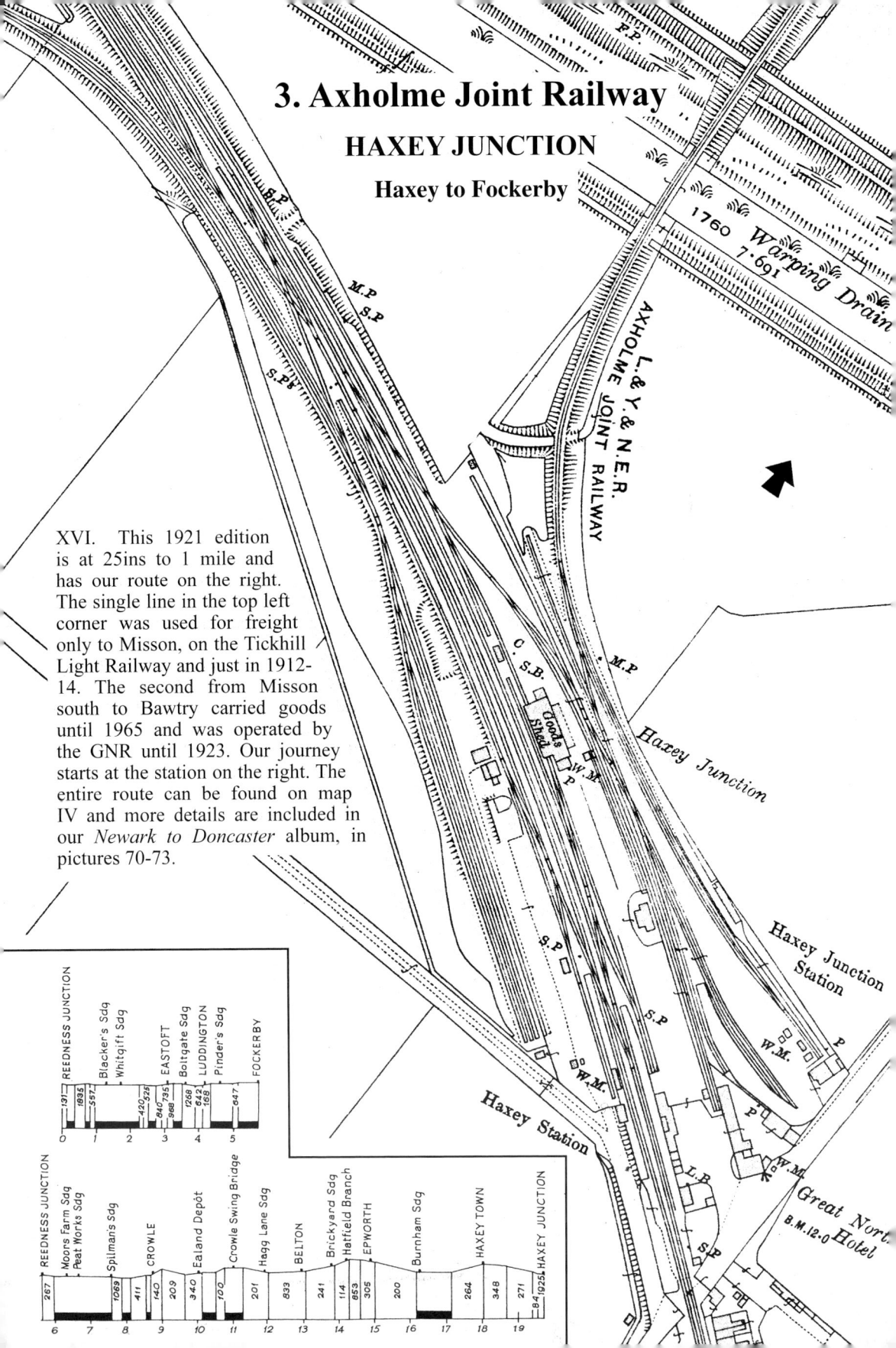

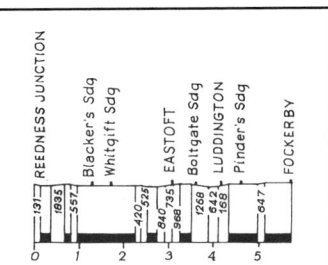

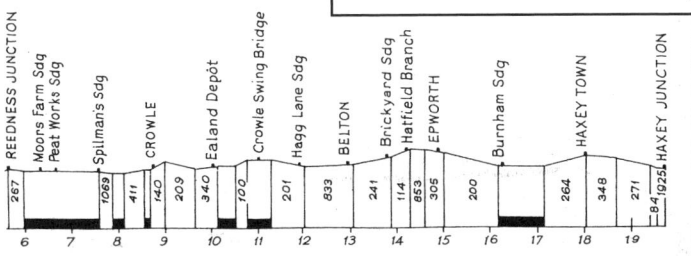

Goods Shed

Haxey Junction

Haxey Junction Station

Haxey Station

Great North. B.M.12.0 Hotel

Upper distance scale:

REEDNESS JUNCTION	Blacker's Sdg	Whitgift Sdg	EASTOFT	Boltgate Sdg	LUDDINGTON	Pinder's Sdg	FOCKERBY
1191 1935 557		420 525	840 735 968	1268 168	642		647

0 1 2 3 4 5

Lower distance scale:

REEDNESS JUNCTION	Moors Farm Sdg	Peat Works Sdg	Spilman's Sdg	CROWLE	Ealand Depôt	Crowle Swing Bridge	Hagg Lane Sdg	BELTON	Brickyard Sdg	Hatfield Branch	EPWORTH	Burnham Sdg	HAXEY TOWN	HAXEY JUNCTION
267			1069	411 140	209	340 100	201	833	241 114	653	305	200	264 348	271 841 1925

6 7 8 9 10 11 12 13 14 15 16 17 18 19

63. This eastward panorama features the terminal platform on the left and the exchange sidings on the right. Blowing off steam is a Sentinel railcar, which was built in Shrewsbury and started work here in December 1930. The first one arrived here in 1926. The levers carry weights to aid manual movement. (J.Alsop coll.)

Views of Haxey station can be found in pictures 78 to 82 in our *Lincoln to Doncaster* **album, in the Middleton Press Eastern Main Lines series. Its map XV has part of the double track across it.**

64. A view after closure to passengers on 15th July 1933 shows the footpath for access from the road and the flat terrain of the district. Clearer here is the white buffer stop at the end of the loop. (SLS coll.)

HAXEY TOWN

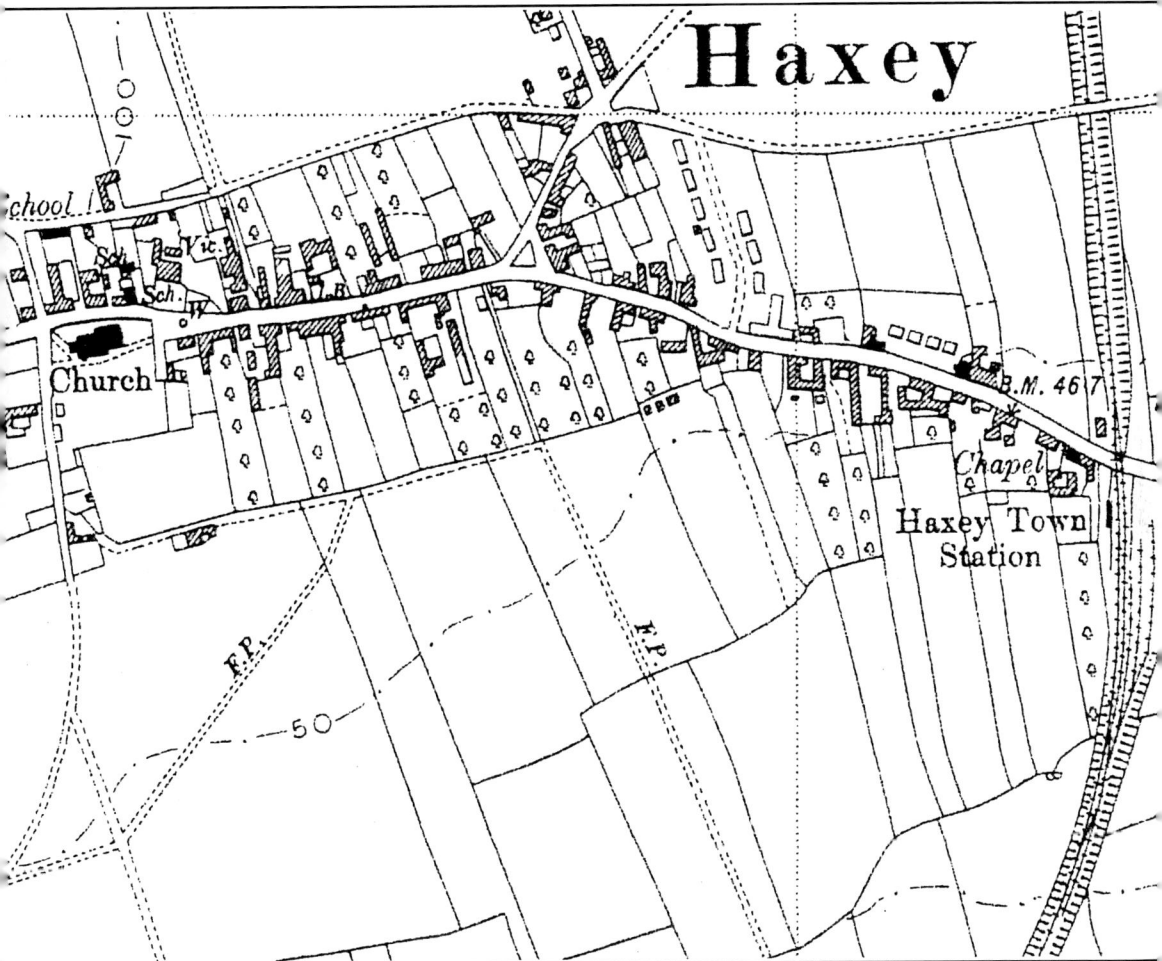

XVII. The second station on the route was 1½ miles from the first, but close to its community. It is seen on the 1949 issue. The residents numbered 2044 in 1901 and 2069 in 1961.

65. Both platforms are evident in this record of a train arriving at too great a speed for the glass plate negative of the time, which was probably about 1905. The bricks are monochrome, except those on the roofless gentleman's area. (J.Alsop coll.)

66. This 1958 southward view is from the level crossing. The chimney on the left is on the right of the previous picture. Passenger traffic had ceased on 15th July 1933 and goods on 1st February 1956. (Stations UK)

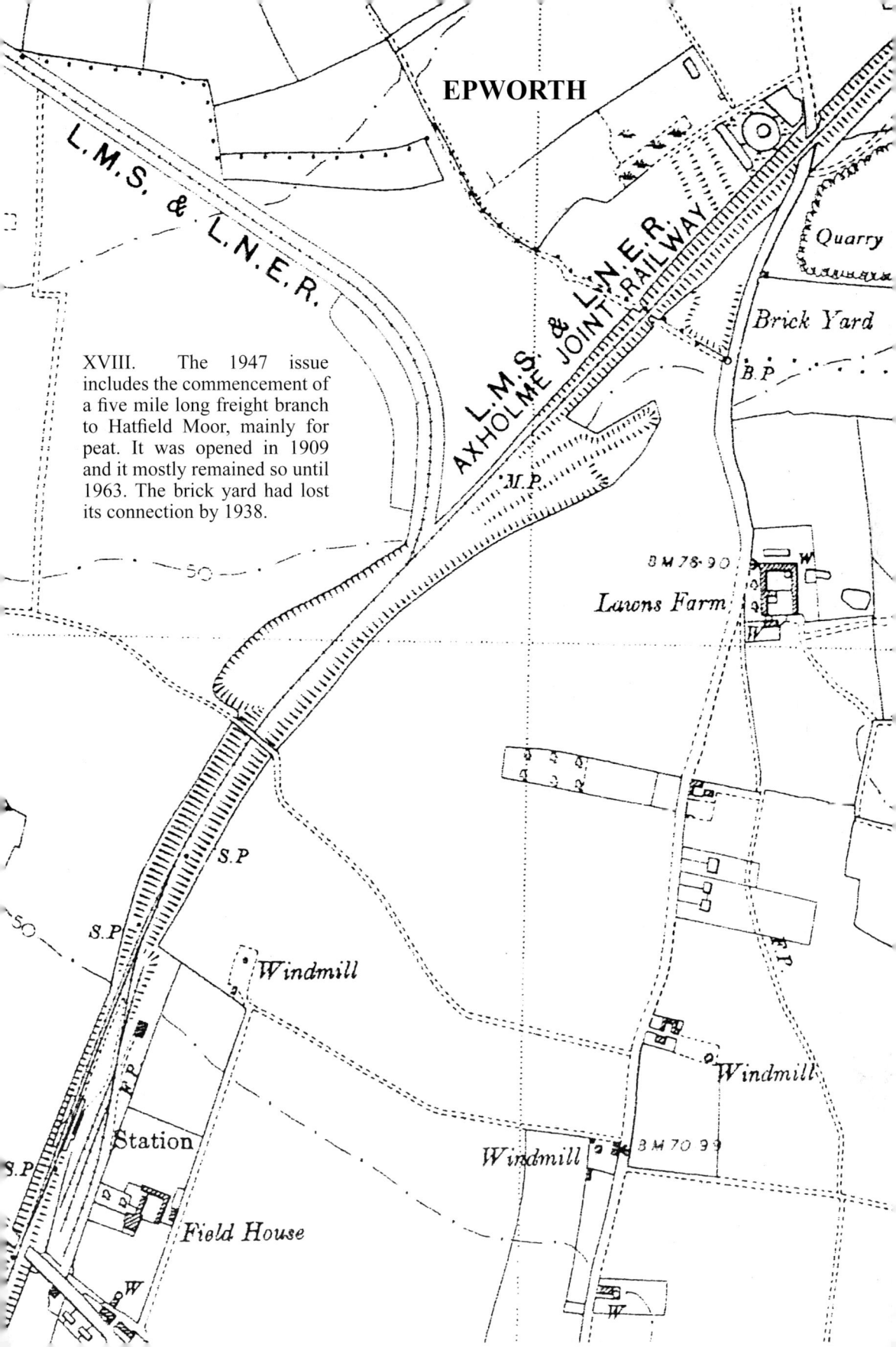

EPWORTH

Quarry

Brick Yard

L.M.S. & L.N.E.R.

L.M.S. & L.N.E.R.
AXHOLME JOINT RAILWAY

B.P.

XVIII. The 1947 issue includes the commencement of a five mile long freight branch to Hatfield Moor, mainly for peat. It was opened in 1909 and it mostly remained so until 1963. The brick yard had lost its connection by 1938.

M.P.

B M 78·90

Lawns Farm

50

S.P.

S.P.

Windmill

Windmill

S.P.

Windmill

B M 70·39

Station

Field House

67. This northward panorama is from the opening year, 1904, while the staff are awaiting name boards. Family members were included by many early photographers. In the background is the outcrop of clay suitable for making bricks. (J.Alsop coll.)

68. This may have been opening day, but excursions to Blackpool in the line's early years were extremely popular. They even continued after routine closure in 1933. The village became famous for the birth of the Wesley brothers, who expanded Christianity with the formation of the Methodist Church, eventually worldwide. Visitor numbers were great, as a result of the completion of the Wesley Memorial Church, nearby. (Stations UK)

69.   This northward view appears to be from the freight-only days, which ended in 1956 southwards and 1966 northwards. On the left is a horse-drawn cart, with its shafts removed. This was just temporary presumably, to facilitate one load transfer. (R.M.Casserley coll.)

70.   Class 05 Hunslet 0-6-0 no. D2611 is heading an enthusiasts' brake van special on 14th September 1963. UK stage history was made in the village in 1981 with the birth in it of Sheridan Smith. She became a noted top star in many fields, internationally. (Colour-Rail.com)

BELTON

XIX. The centre of Belton was ½ mile south of the station, which is shown on the 1907 issue at 25ins to 1 mile. It closed to passengers on 15th July 1933.

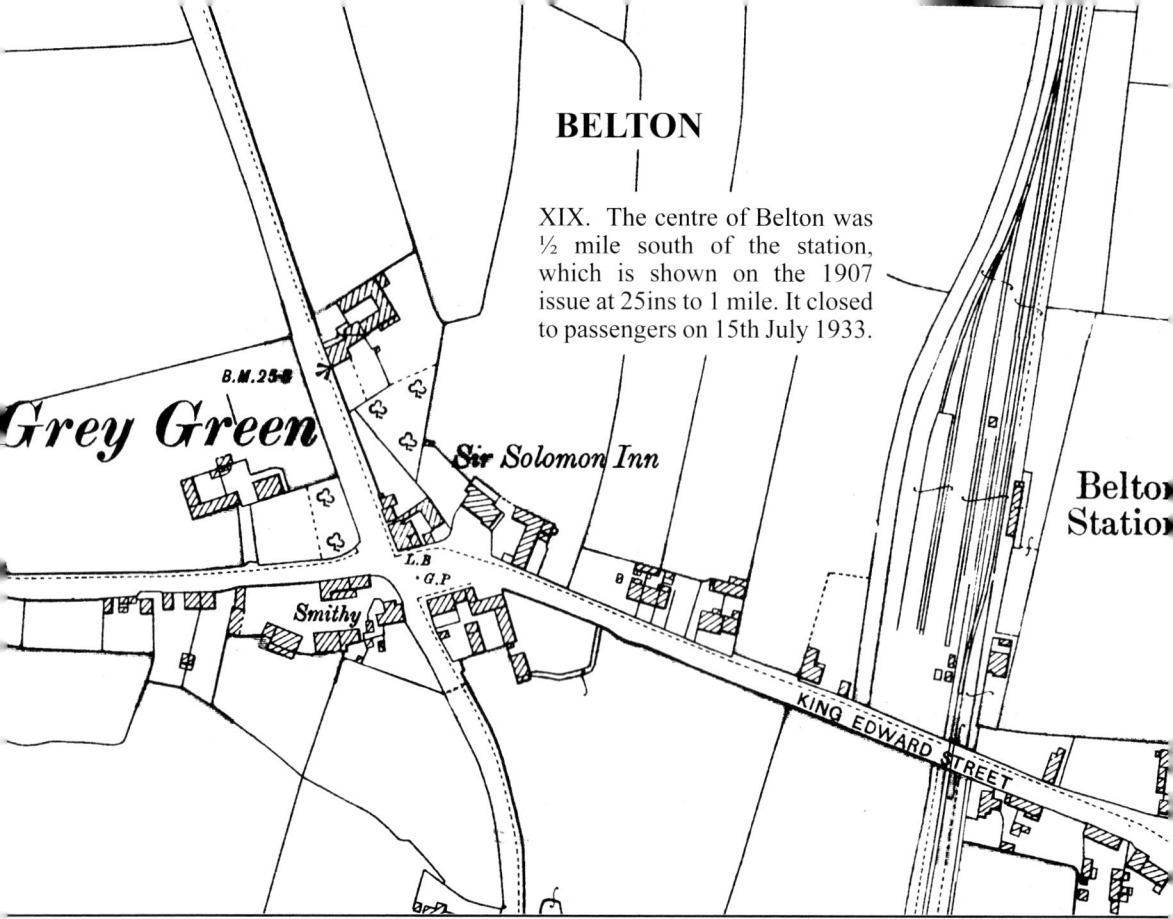

Grey Green

Sir Solomon Inn

B.M.25·8

L.B
·G.P

Smithy

Belton Station

KING EDWARD STREET

71. The level crossing is seen in the construction period, before the gates were fitted and before the station master's curtains had arrived. The 1901 census showed 1482 residents in the district. (J.Alsop coll.)

CHAMBERLAIN'S TRAIN, BELTON STATION.

72. The low level of the platform is evident in this view. We have tried to find the significance of 'Chamberlain's Train', but with no luck. The loop and other platform (up) came into use in February 1907. The station carried the suffix of FOR WEST BUTTERWICK for a period. (J.Alsop coll.)

73. The second platform and the crossing to it are centre in this 1958 panorama. The building on the left is the weigh house and goods office. Freight traffic ceased here on 5th April 1965. Sugar beet had been a large part of it. (Stations UK)

74. Crowle Swing Bridge and span passed over the main line and the Stainforth & Keadby Canal, two miles from Belton station and two miles before reaching Crowle (AJR). The 12-arch viaduct also passed over rivers: the New Idle, the Double, the Torne and the Folly Drain. The 12-lever signal box (left) was in use until 1951, when Crowle Crossing Box took over. (R.Humm coll.)

AXHOLME JOINT RAILWAY.
THIRD CLASS
FOCKERBY
TO
HULL(NE)
via Staddlethorpe
Available on day of issue only
TURN OVER   Fare 2s11d
E 28 05
33

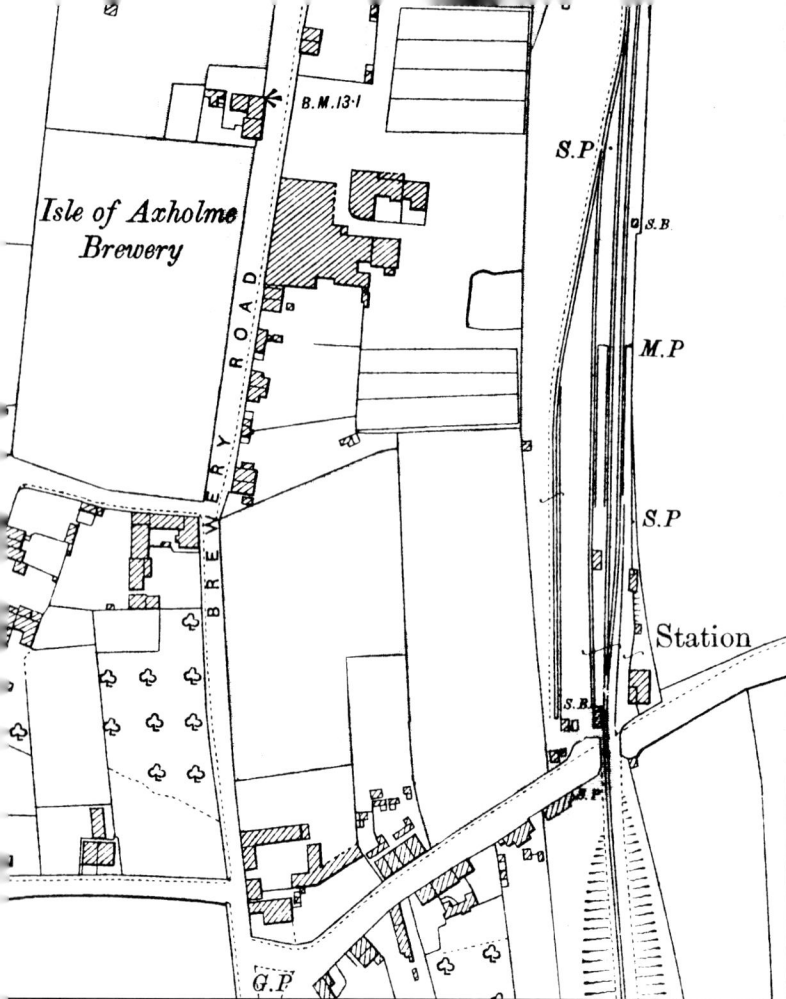

CROWLE (AJR)

XX. Although the GCR station had the suffix CENTRAL for a long period, this one was just known as TOWN locally and AJR when necessary. Pictures 26 to 31 show the other one and map IV has both. The one here is based on the 1907 edition and is at 20ins to 1 mile.

75. This fine northward panorama includes the weighbridge in front of its office on the left and also horse traction, then universal. A ground frame was situated in the small building centre, to the left of the level crossing. The coal office is probably on the right, where domestic sales would be undertaken. It might have also acted as a stable. (J.Alsop coll.)

76. The ticket office was part of the station masters house. On the left is the waiting room on the path to the down platform. There was a waiting shelter on the other one. In reality, the house was occupied for its first 23 years by the superintendent of the AJR. (P.Laming coll.)

77. One of the Sentinel railcars is signalled to depart north. The chimney on its vertical boiler is at its far end. The hut on the right was the lamp room, where wicks were trimmed and oil filling took place. Closure dates were: passengers 15th July 1933 and freight 5th April 1965. (J.Alsop coll.)

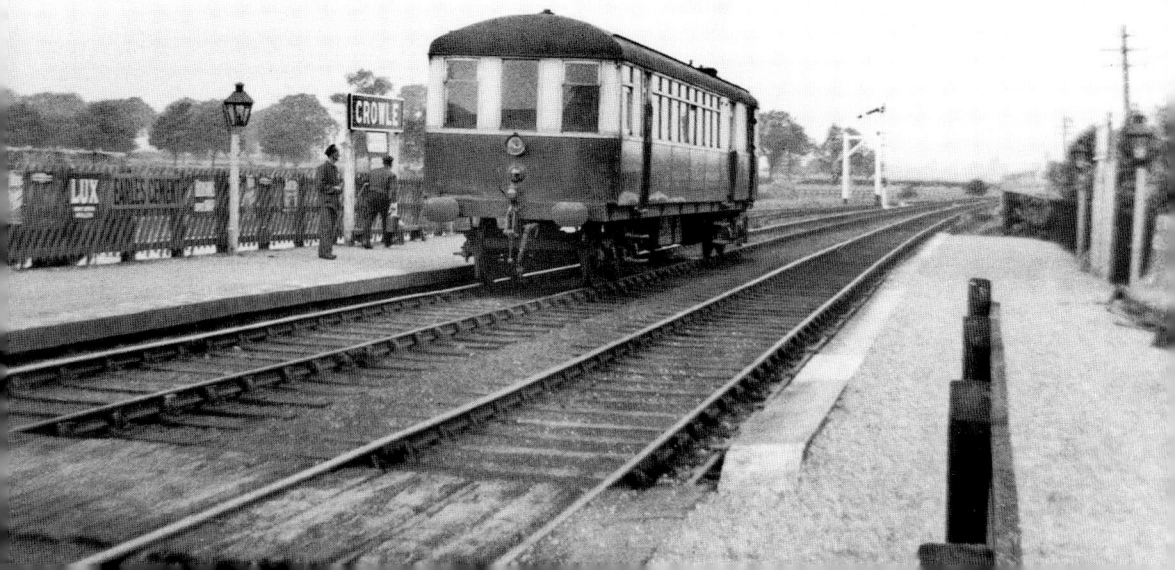

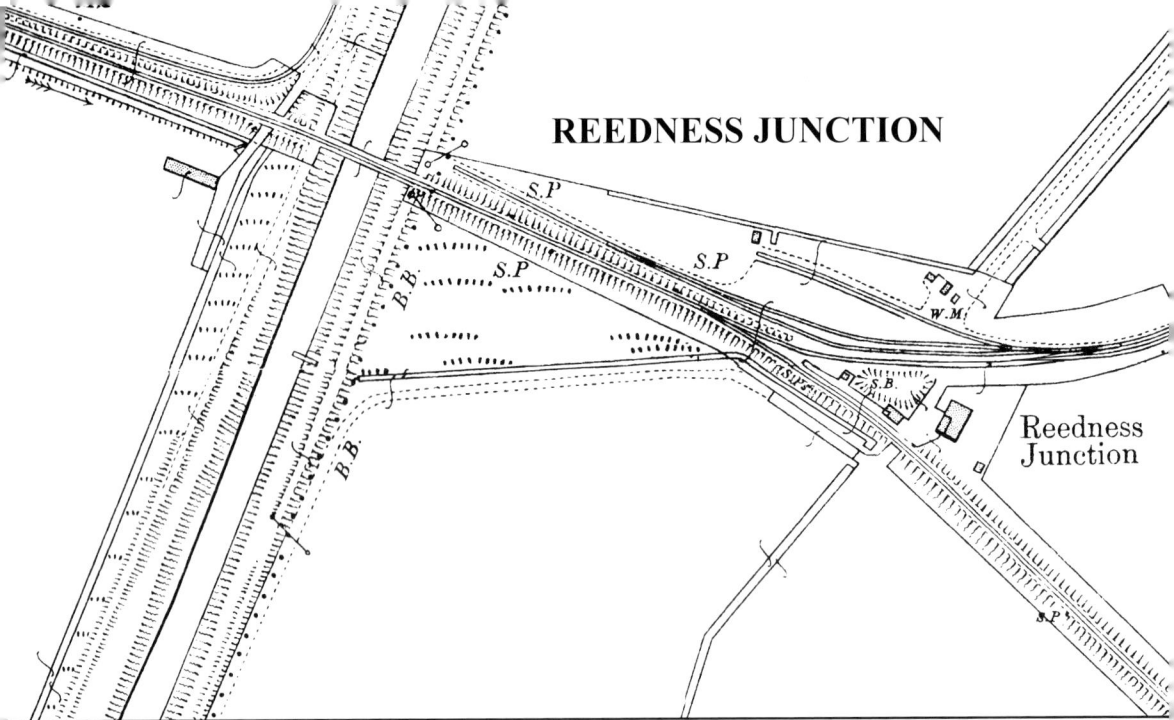

REEDNESS JUNCTION

Reedness
Junction

XXI. The 1914 issue is at 25ins to 1 mile. Our route from Haxey is lower right and the platform for Fockerby trains is close to the right border. The Goole line is top left and passes over the Swinefleet Warping Drain.

78.   Reedness Junction was reached after passing two sidings for local agricultural traffic called 'Ealand Depot'. They were about 1½ miles from Crowle. Yorkshire Peat Works siding followed. It was on the west side of the line and had a 3ft gauge railway, which was several miles long. A railcar from Haxey waits to leave for Goole. (J.Alsop coll.)

79.   Beyond the water column is the lever box, which was worked by station staff, not a signalman. The platform positions are shown on the map. A small child waits for Hunslet diesel 0-6-0 no. D2600 to depart, in the early 1960s. Closure dates are as shown in caption 77; they apply to the next three stations. (Colour-Rail.com)

AXHOLME JOINT RAILWAY.
THIRD CLASS
BELTON
TO
GOOLE(N.E)
Available on day of issue only
33
G
TURN OVER   Fare 1s1d
NO 80.05   460

AXHOLME JOINT RAILWAY.
Issued subject to the regulations & conditions
in the Co's Time Tables. Books. Bills & Notices
CROWLE   TO
GOOLE(L.N.E.)
THIRD CLASS   2327   (S)   Fare 1/1½
GOOLE
MR 9 '28   9496

AXHOLME JOINT RAILWAY.
Issued subject to the conditions & regulations in
the Co's Time Tables Books Bills & Notices& in the
Railway Cos Book of regulations relating to traffic
by Passenger Train or other similar Service
REEDNESS JUNC.   TO
CROWLE
THIRD CLASS   2323 (S) FARE -/4½
CROWLE
8569

AXHOLME JOINT RAILWAY.
THIRD CLASS
REEDNESS JUNCTION
TO
GOOLE
Available on day of issue only.
TURN OVER   Fare 5½d.
80 SP 05   27

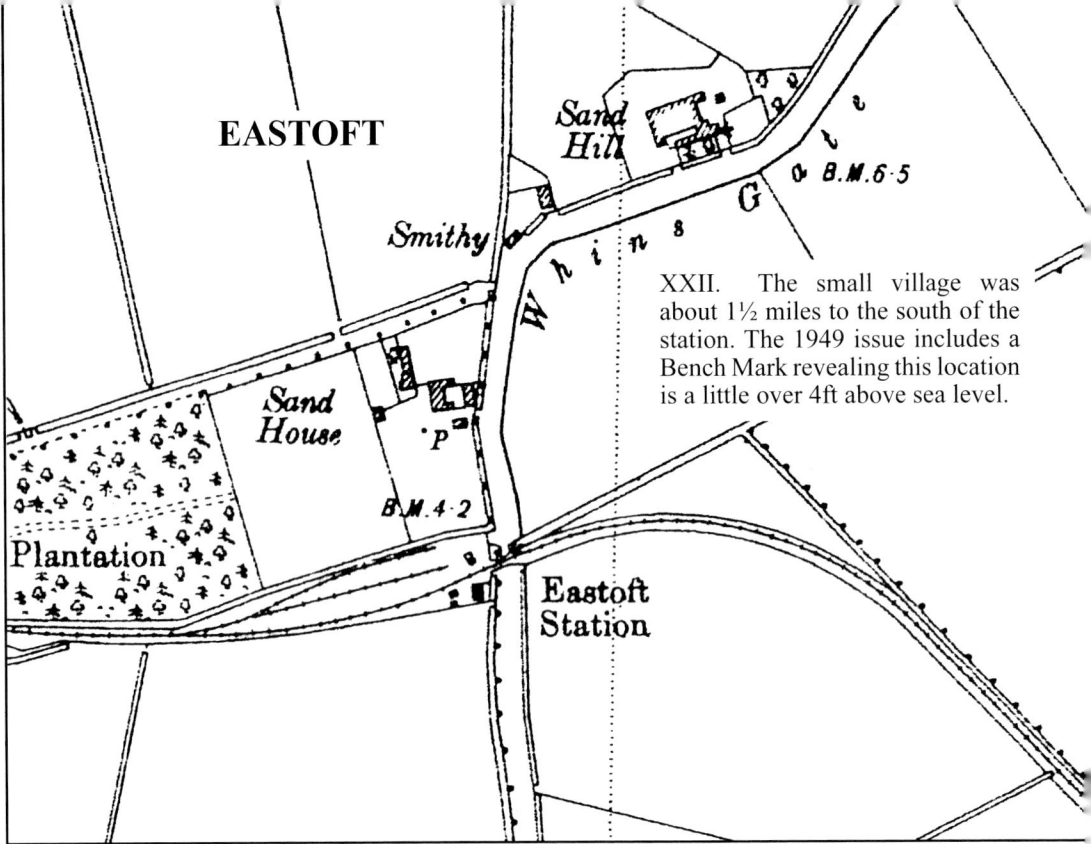

EASTOFT

Sand Hill

Smithy

Whins G ○ B.M.6·5

Sand House

·P·

B.M.4·2

Plantation

Eastoft Station

XXII.   The small village was about 1½ miles to the south of the station. The 1949 issue includes a Bench Mark revealing this location is a little over 4ft above sea level.

80.   Class 2 2-6-0 no. 46478 waits near to the level crossing in the early 1960s, not long before route closure in 1965. It obscures the station building and platform, but the goods office is evident on the right. Flat land is beyond. (Photos from the Fifties)

LUDDINGTON

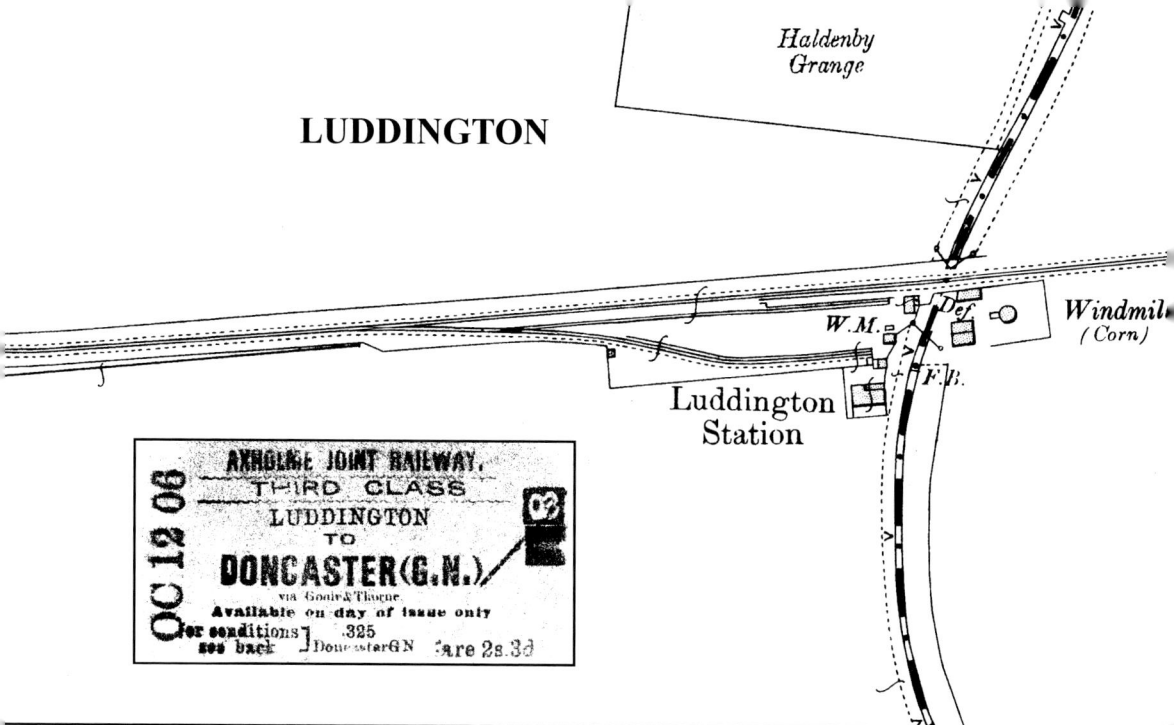

Haldenby Grange

Windmill (Corn)

W.M.

Luddington
Station

F.B.

AXHOLME JOINT RAILWAY.
THIRD CLASS
LUDDINGTON
TO
DONCASTER(G.N.)
via Goole & Thorne.
Available on day of issue only
For conditions] .325
see back] Doncaster GN Fare 2s.3d

OC 12 06

XXIII. This 25ins scale map was dated 1906 and includes the dots and dashes of the county boundary. In 1938, there were private sidings listed here for Boltgate and Pinders, but the traffic was not detailed. F.B. refers to a footbridge over the stream. It is close to the station masters house.

81. This June 1958 view still includes the ticket office hatch, although it had closed 25 years earlier. The goods service would continue for another seven years. The fire buckets indicate that staff were still present, at least part-time. They hang on the small signal box, which was disused. (J.Suter coll.)

FOCKERBY

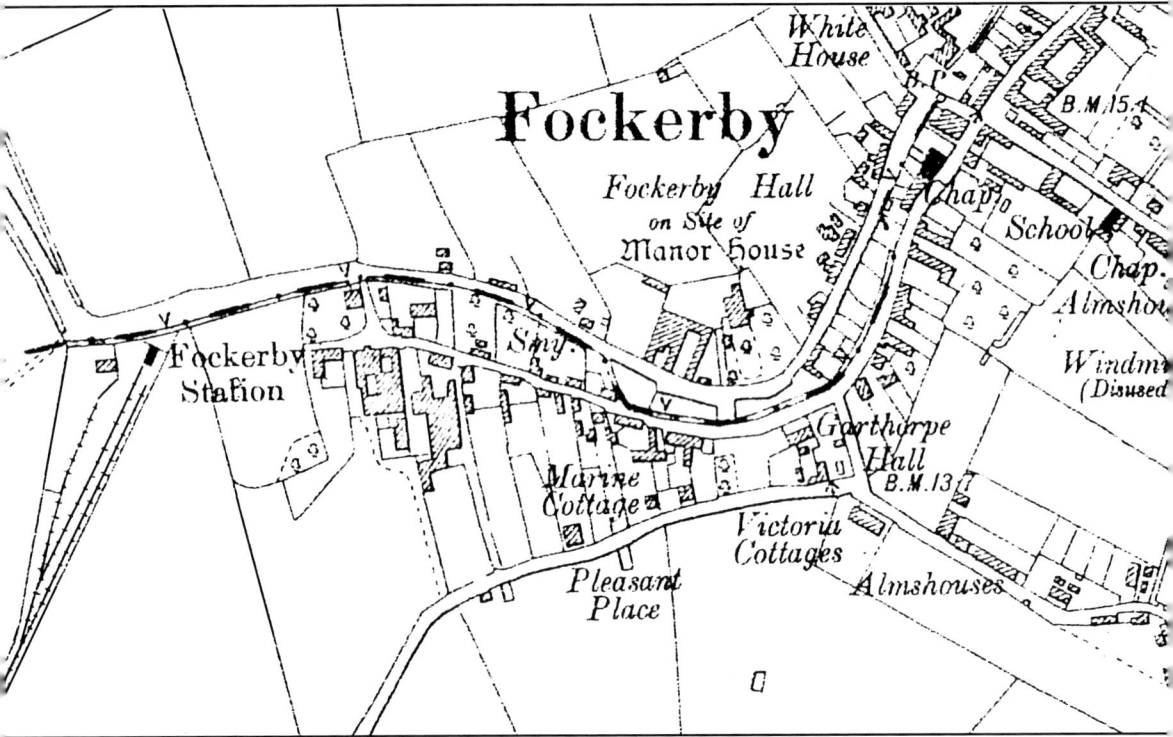

XXIV. Shown in black in the station area is the main building, and hatched is the house for the station master. The crossover is not on this 1908 edition. The boundary meant that only 74 lived in Fockerby in 1901, but 481 resided in adjacent Garthorpe, mostly just over the road.

82. The coal wagon suggests that this is probably a pre-1923 view. It features the missing crossover and L&YR 0-6-0 no. 954. This was built by Beyer Peacock in 1887. (LOSA)

83. A well-lit view from 13th August 1960 reveals all to be in good condition. The entrance to the main building was on its far side, with a path from the lane. (Colour-Rail.com)

84. The weekday freight service was recorded on 22nd July 1961, but the details were not. The passenger platform was close to the fence, but was not used after 15th July 1933. Freight ended on 5th April 1965. (H.Davies coll.)

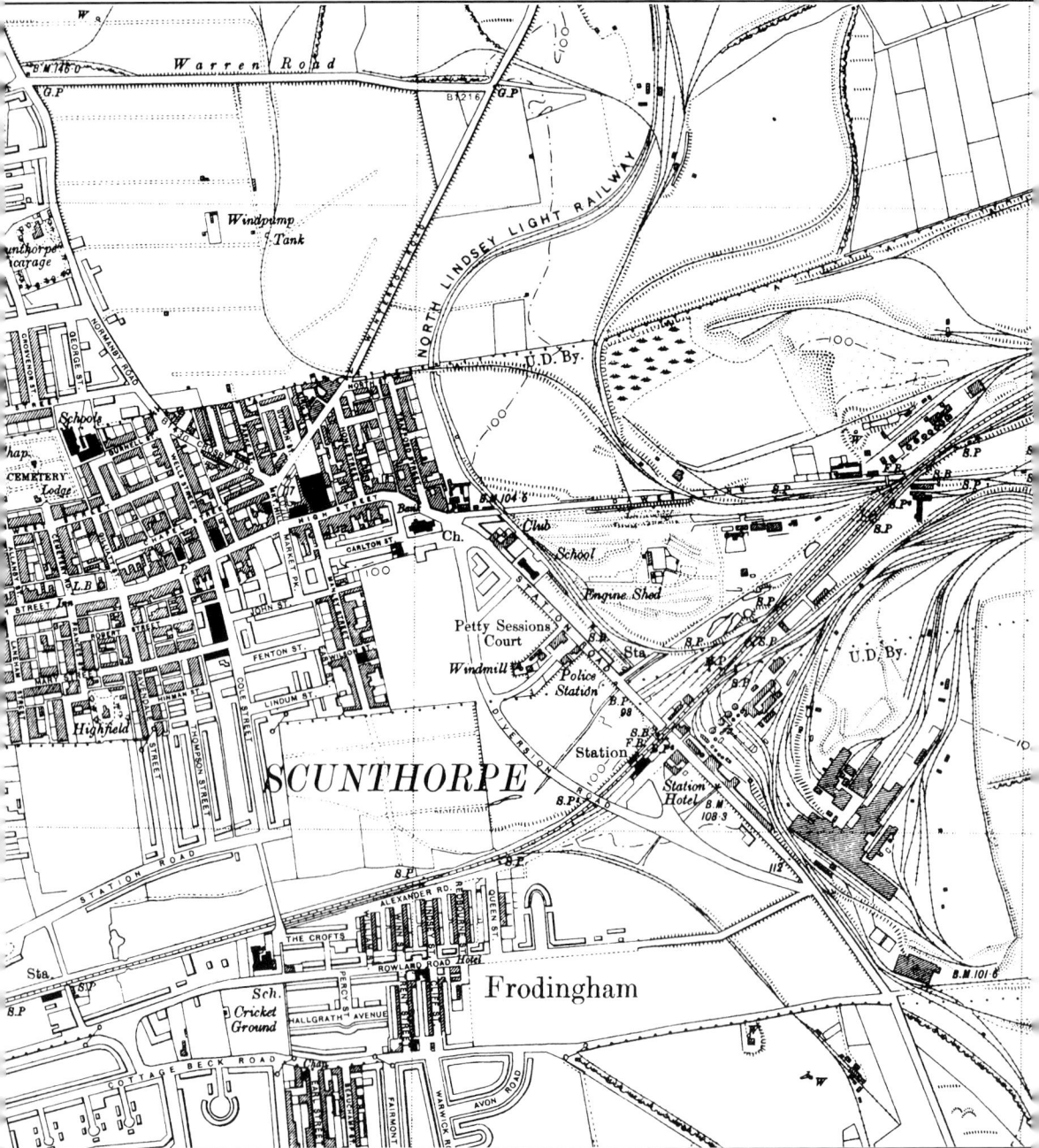

4. North Lindsey Light Railway

Whitton Branch

SCUNTHORPE (NLLR)

Gradient profile:

Juncⁿ with G.C. R^y at Frodingham. — Winterton & Thealby Stⁿ — West Halton Stⁿ — Winteringham Stⁿ

| 110 | 396 | 286 | 154 | 462 | 770 | 352 | 14·08 | 924 | 550 | 1188 | 1056 | 1122 | 1628 | 198 | 14·08 | 1386 | 693 | 572 |

| 1 in 108 | 1 in 560 | 1 in 104 | Level | 1 in 133 | Level | 1 in 55 | 1 in 127 | 1 in 354 | 1 in 121 | 1 in 109 | 1 in 177 | 1 in 306 | 1 in 577 | Level | 1 in 498 | 1 in 272 | 1 in 550 | Level |

SCUNTHORPE

Frodingham

XXV. The 1906 railway is named near the top of this 1938 issue and its terminal station is centre, below 'Engine Shed'. A little further south is the station on the main line and near the left border is Scunthorpe & Frodingham station, which had opened on 11th March 1928, replacing Frodingham & Scunthorpe, which is still shown, near the Station Hotel. The name details are given in captions 7 and 8. The route north is shown on map V. The 1932 LNER engine shed is near the right border, north of the main line.

85. This was recorded as the first train to leave and the date is 3rd September 1906, but the terminus is totally obscured. A GCR class 6C 0-6-0 is seen; 'Jumbo' and 'Bulldog' were names applied by some to that class. (J.Alsop coll.)

86. At the terminal platform in about 1908 are two GCR six-wheeled coaches, plus *Cawood*. This was no. 6, a Manning Wardle 'Special L' 0-6-0ST, works no. 1360 of 1897. (J.Alsop coll.)

Dawes Lane

87. Seen on 5th May 1975 are details not always included: the small windows of the machine room, the rodding tunnel below them and the coal store for box heating. Dawes Lane is shown twice on diagram XXX; this one was north of the main line and shown as an automated crossing. The 30-lever box opened on 18th August 1912 and closed on 22nd September 1985. (N.D.Mundy)

Crosby Mines

88. The first box opened on 31st July 1906 and closed 15th August 1913. It had 22 levers. The second Crosby Mines signal box is seen in the early 1970s. This was a key location for moving ore from opencast mines north of Scunthorpe to the local iron and steelworks. Seldom recorded is the private toilet used by box staff only. Their box opened on 15th August 1913, closed on 13th September 1991 and had 30 levers. The brick base was provided in the 1950s; the box would have been all-timber originally. (N.Fisher)

Normanby Park

89.   An overhead conveyor flanks the box roof. The line branching left beyond the box continued to Flixborough Wharf on the River Trent. The village name is on map IV. (R.Turner)

Flixborough Wharf

90.   Some maps describe the location as Flixborough Stather. No. 5 was a 'Janus' class from Yorkshire Engine Co. as no. 2909/63. It is at work on 3rd June 1981. The site had become busy with imported iron ore. (R.Humm coll.)

WINTERTON & THEALBY

B.M.34·1

B

S.B.

Winterton & Thealby Station

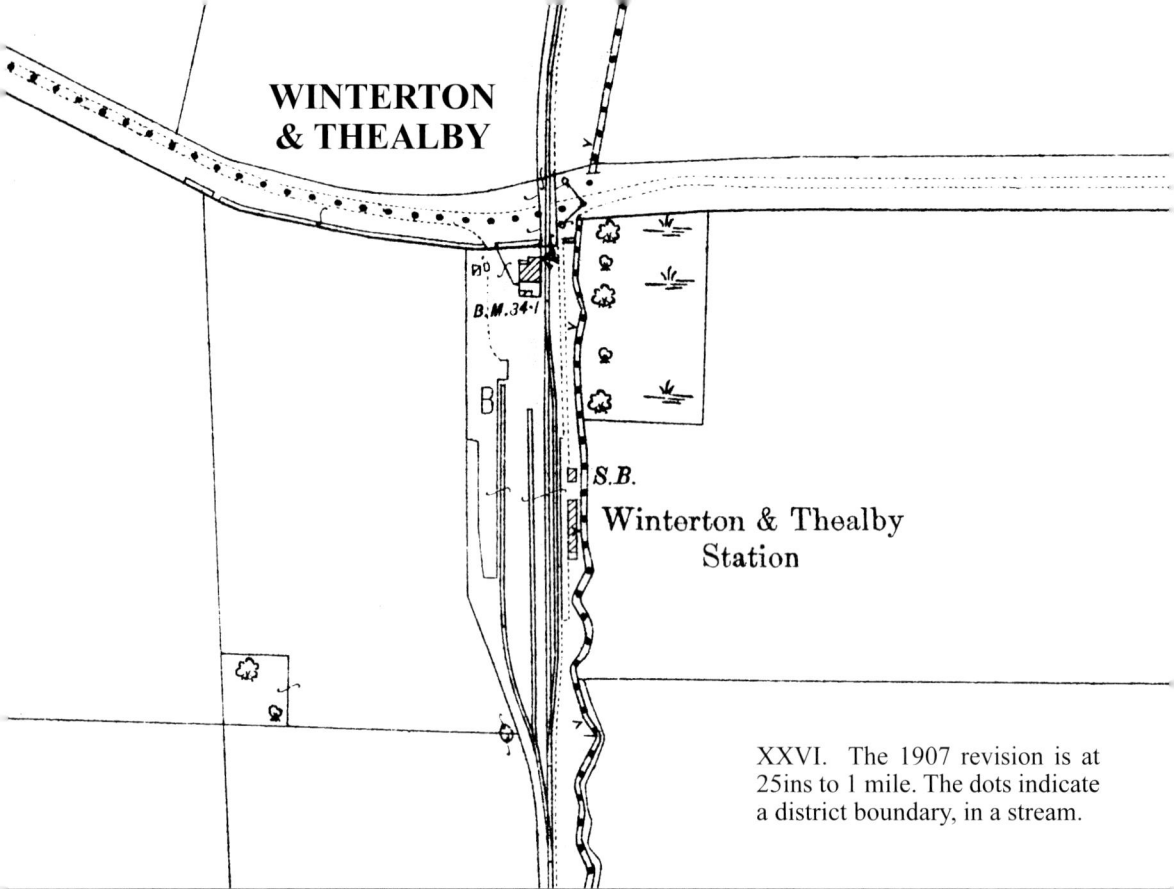

XXVI. The 1907 revision is at 25ins to 1 mile. The dots indicate a district boundary, in a stream.

91. The first train was recorded again on 3rd September 1906. The 12-lever signal box was listed as opening on 31st July 1906 and having the levers reduced to five by 1921. (P.Laming coll.)

92.   The buildings were photographed in the early 1960s, the line northwards having closed totally on 29th May 1961. Light Railways could have very low platforms, as seen. The town can be found on map IV, where it is shown to be about one mile east of the station. The goods yard was still busy in September 1962; closure came on 20th July 1964. (Industrial Railway Society)

93.   Class K1 2-6-0 no. 62035 waits with the Railway Enthusiasts Club 'North Lindseyman' special train of brake vans on 21st April 1963. All the track has old bullhead rail visible. (Photos from the Fifties)

WEST HALTON

West Halton Sidings

XXVII. The northern terminus of the route was here from 3rd September 1906 until 15th July 1907. This 1949 edition shows no evidence of a loop line. Records show an 18-lever box initially, its number having been reduced to eight by 1933.

94. The RCTS railtour on 20th June 1954 stopped for members to examine the remains. Haulage was by ex-GCR class J11 0-6-0 no. 64419. Members are blurred due to their movement on an old slow film speed. (Photos from the Fifties)

WINTERINGHAM

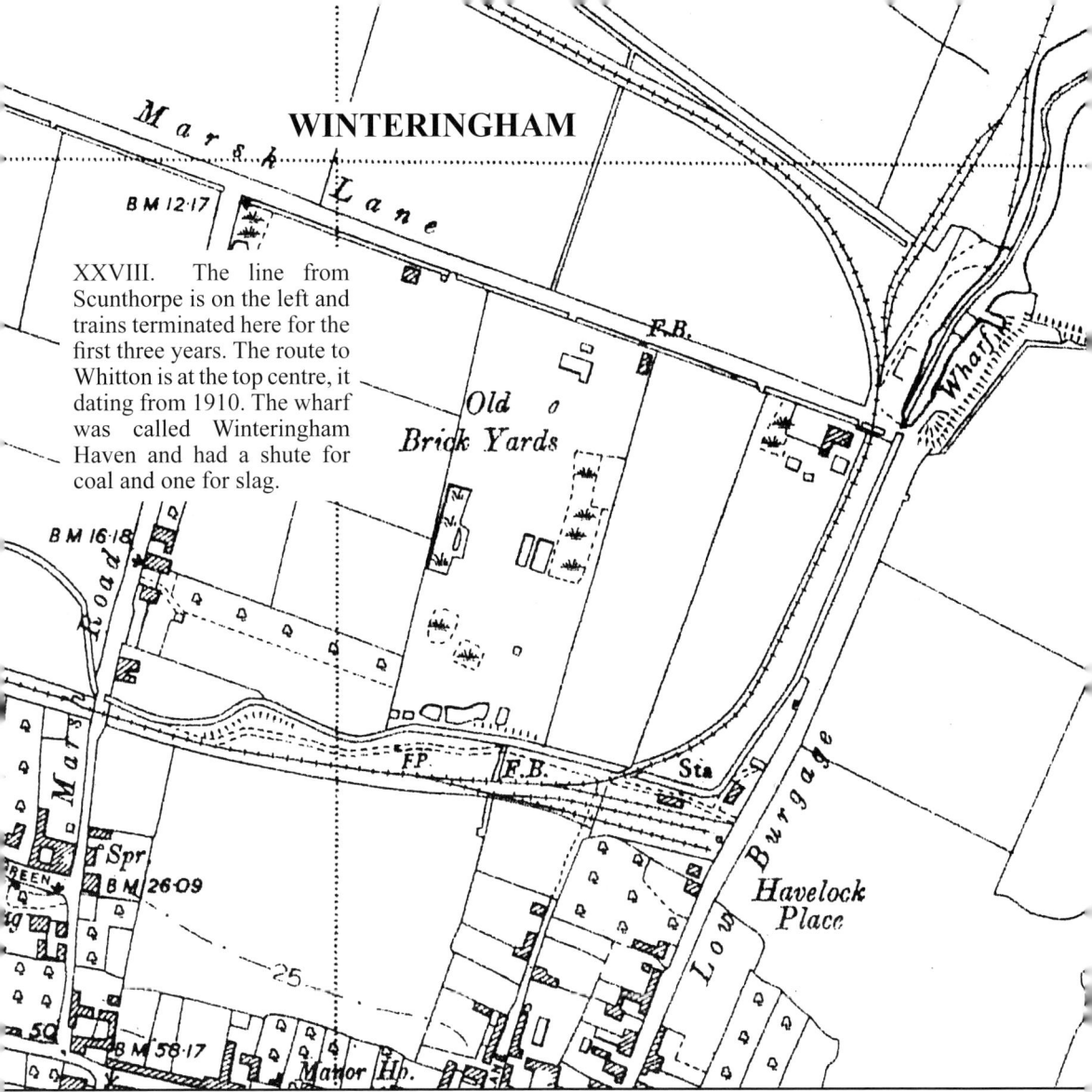

XXVIII. The line from Scunthorpe is on the left and trains terminated here for the first three years. The route to Whitton is at the top centre, it dating from 1910. The wharf was called Winteringham Haven and had a shute for coal and one for slag.

Old Brick Yards

95. The first train is seen on 15th July 1907, with status by hat still prevalent. There was a ferry to Hull on Mondays and one back on Fridays. Residents numbered 595 in the 1901 census. The loco is a GCR 0-6-2T. (R.Humm coll.)

96. The date on the picture was given as 'by February 1909', but no name boards had been supplied. There is safety fencing on the right. This prevented doors being opened there. (J.Alsop coll.)

97. The departure signals are beyond the goods dock. No signal box was provided, the six levers being in a ground frame. The block post was held inside the station. It was out of use by 1951. Total closure came on 20th July 1964. (R.Humm coll.)

WHITTON

Old Gravel Pits

Whitton

St. John the Baptist's Church

Chapel

Manor House

Smithy

The Grange

XXIX. The village housed 173 folk in 1901 and they had a train service from 1st December 1910 until 13th July 1925. The name did not conflict with the Whitton near Hounslow, as that station did not open until 1930. This map is from 1951. Top left is the Whitton Channel of the River Humber.

98. The terminus is seen in its early days. It handled goods until 1st October 1951. There was no signal box, just a one-lever ground frame. (J.Alsop coll.)

5. Scunthorpe Steelworks Area

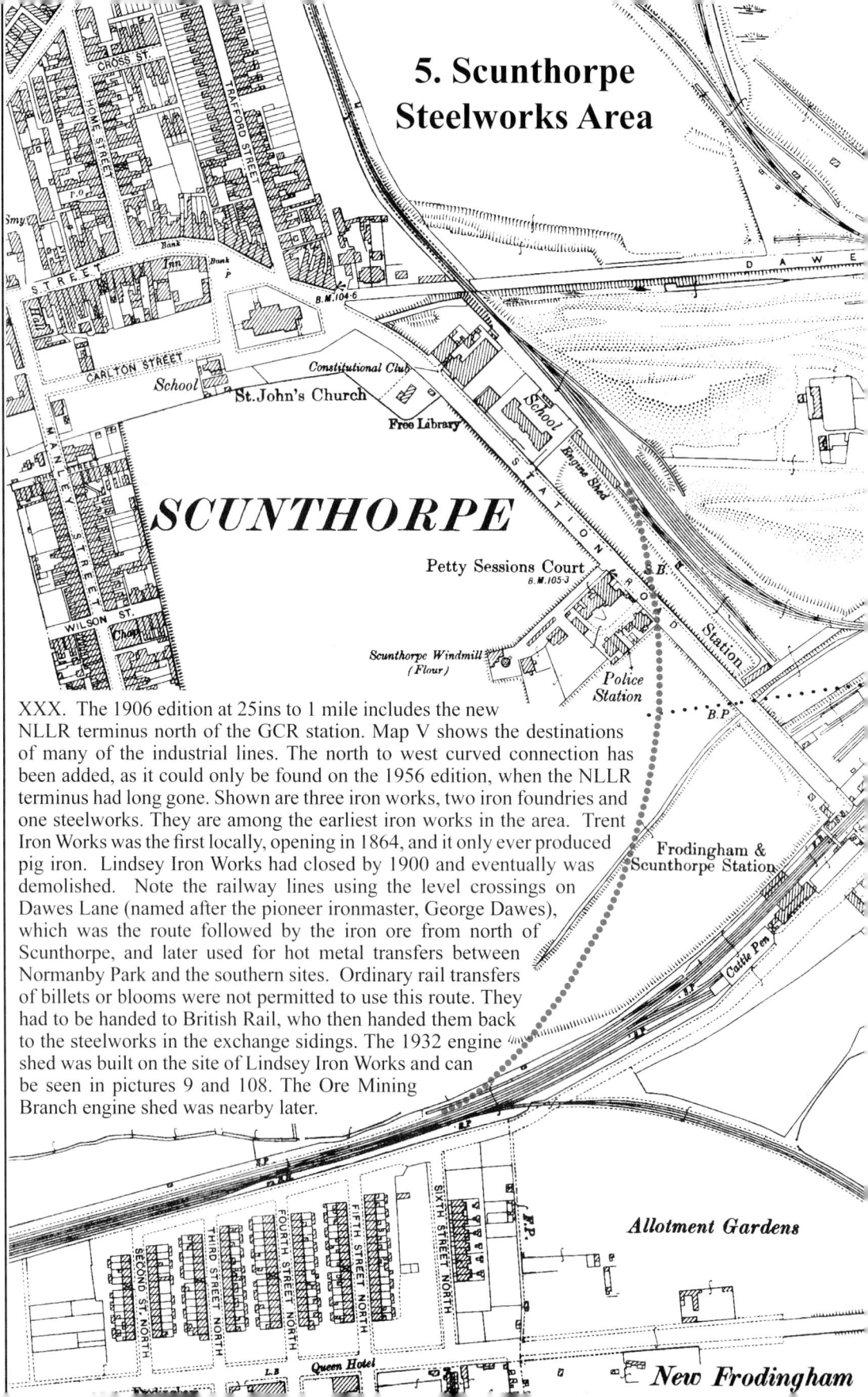

CROSS ST.

HOME STREET

TRAFFORD STREET

Smy.

P.O.

Bank

Street Inn

Bank

STREET

CARLTON STREET

School

MANLEY STREET

WILSON ST.

Chap.

B.M.104·6

Constitutional Club

St. John's Church

Free Library

School

Engine Shed

Scunthorpe Windmill
(Flour)

SCUNTHORPE

Petty Sessions Court
B.M.105·3

STATION ROAD

Station

DAWE

B.

Police Station

B.P.

Frodingham & Scunthorpe Station

Castle Pen

Allotment Gardens

XXX. The 1906 edition at 25ins to 1 mile includes the new NLLR terminus north of the GCR station. Map V shows the destinations of many of the industrial lines. The north to west curved connection has been added, as it could only be found on the 1956 edition, when the NLLR terminus had long gone. Shown are three iron works, two iron foundries and one steelworks. They are among the earliest iron works in the area. Trent Iron Works was the first locally, opening in 1864, and it only ever produced pig iron. Lindsey Iron Works had closed by 1900 and eventually was demolished. Note the railway lines using the level crossings on Dawes Lane (named after the pioneer ironmaster, George Dawes), which was the route followed by the iron ore from north of Scunthorpe, and later used for hot metal transfers between Normanby Park and the southern sites. Ordinary rail transfers of billets or blooms were not permitted to use this route. They had to be handed to British Rail, who then handed them back to the steelworks in the exchange sidings. The 1932 engine shed was built on the site of Lindsey Iron Works and can be seen in pictures 9 and 108. The Ore Mining Branch engine shed was nearby later.

SIXTH STREET NORTH

FIFTH STREET NORTH

FOURTH STREET NORTH

THIRD STREET NORTH

SECOND ST. NORTH

F.P.

L.B.

Queen Hotel

New Frodingham

Trent Iron Works

n Foundry

Lindsey
Iron Works
(Disused)

Iron
Foundry

G. C. R.
BARNSLEY TO BARNETBY

U. D. Bdy.

Def.

Frodingham
Iron & Steel Work

llotment Gardens

Chemical Works

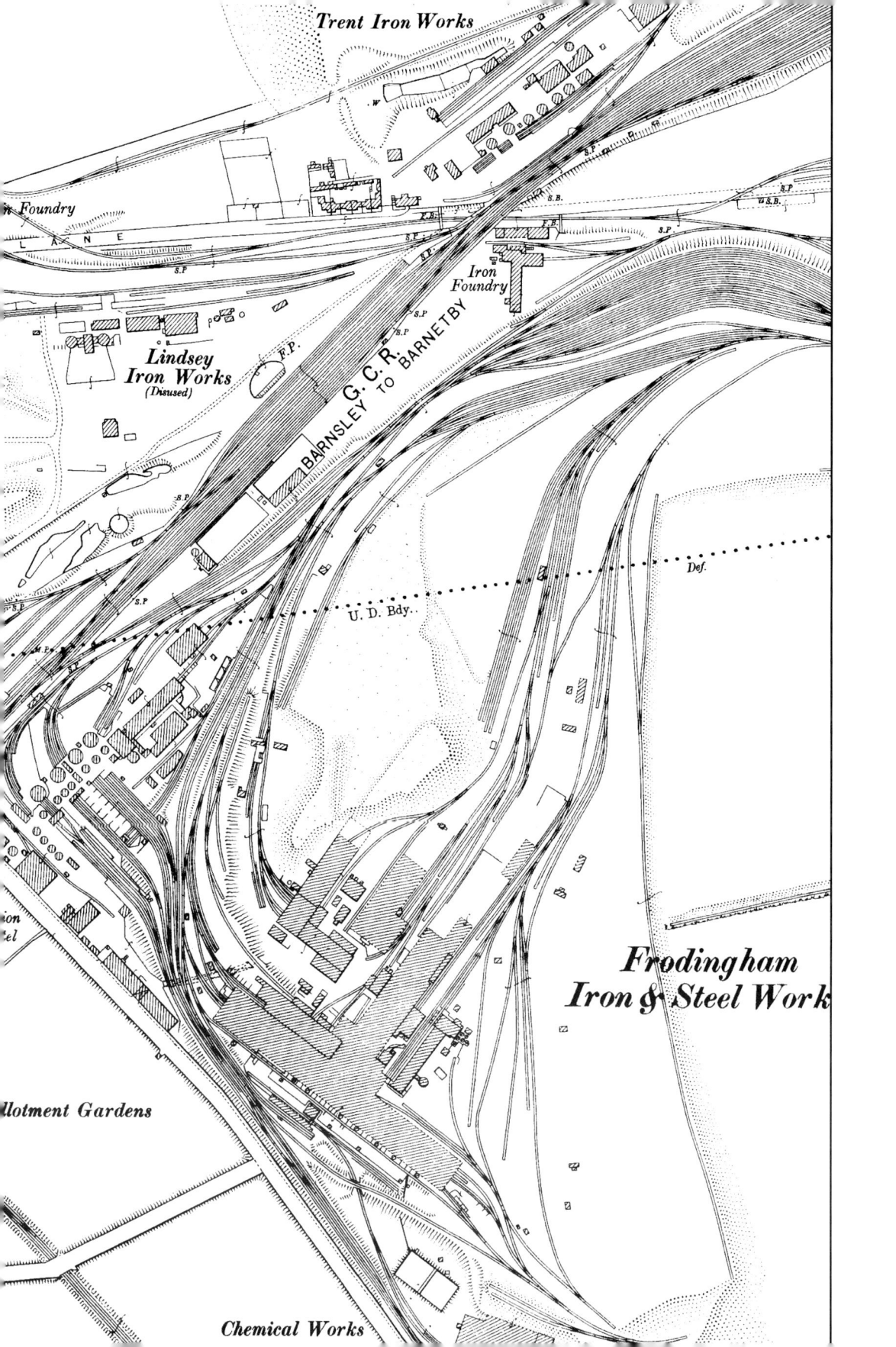

Railway track diagram labels (top to bottom, left to right):

- • (Crosby Mines) 1.45
- NOP
- a = (Dawes Lane Jn)
- b = Trent Jn 0.00/23.51
- Freight Sidings EWS
- SCD
- COM 0.25 / 0.28
- Dawes Lane (AOCL) 0.32
- Grant Rail OTM
- Corus Coal Handling Plant
- Hopper & Control Panel
- A ARRIVAL / RECEPTION SDGS / DEPARTURE ROAD / STANDAGE DOCK
- Cripple Sdgs
- Santon Ore Mining (32A) 25.11
- (7) SCUNTHORPE 22.54
- Scunthorpe West Jn 23.13
- No. 2 REC / No. 1 REC
- UP SCUNTHORPE GDS
- UP SCUNTHORPE
- UP MAIN / DOWN MAIN
- Nth Lincoln Jn 24.25
- Foreign Ore Branch Jn 25.34
- 22.29 / 22.33 / E LINE
- UP MAIN / DOWN MAIN / No. 1 RECEPTION
- DOWN SCUNTHORPE GDS
- TRANSFER 23.40 / TRANSFER 23.65
- DN SCUNTHORPE GOODS
- TRENT RECEPTION LINE 24.10
- UP SC G / DN SC.G
- UP SCUNTHORPE GOODS
- 24.55 / 0.00
- Scunthorpe (S) 23.27
- SSH
- High Yd
- Trent Sdgs EWS
- Low Yd OOU
- AN 3 (ECCLES)
- 'C' Ent
- Eccles Sdgs Qy
- Anchor Exchange Sidings BS / 1-3 inwards / 4 Loco release & Loop Sdg. / 5-15 Outwards
- SCUNTHORPE FOREIGN ORE BRANCH
- SAN [LN 754]
- Santon Foreign Ore Branch 0.25
- Old Station
- No. 7 BAY / No. 6 BAY
- North Lincoln Sdgs
- Structural Workshops
- Wagon Shops
- No. 2 Pit Arch
- Dawes Lane
- North Lincoln Sidings (left to right) / Middle Line / Old Back / Middle Back / Far Back
- A Sdgs
- No. 1 Pit Arch
- Heavy Plate Mill
- Ent 'B' / Ent 'B' Sdgs
- Container Terminal
- Ore Tippler Plant 0.69
- CR 0.50
- Muck Bank
- Mills Exchange Sidings Qy
- HRB = Heavy Repair Bay
- APPLEBY-FRODINGHAM Railway Preservation Society Excursion Platform 'Frodingham'
- Heavy Section Mill
- Frodingham Stripper
- Ent 'D' Sdgs
- Foreign Ore Terminal 1.16
- WB's
- TIPPLER LINE
- Loco Shed 'Appleby'
- Appleby Coke Ovens
- Quench Car Track
- ORE BEDS
- North Lincoln Road
- APPLEBY - FRODINGHAM WORKS Corus
- Rod Mill
- Torpedo Repair Bay
- Blast Furnaces
- Sinter Plant 60-70 Group
- Scrap Recovery & Iron Ponds
- Platelayers Stock Ground
- Bloom & Billet Mills
- Medium Section Mill
- HIGH LINE
- CC = Continuous Casting
- BOS = Basic Oxygen Steel
- Slab Bay
- 20 Group Sdgs
- Northants Bridge
- Molten Metal Traffic Control Cabin OOU
- Bridge 44
- Mould Shop
- CC / BOS / Scrap Bay
- OUTWARDS / INWARDS 22.50
- Former Entrance E

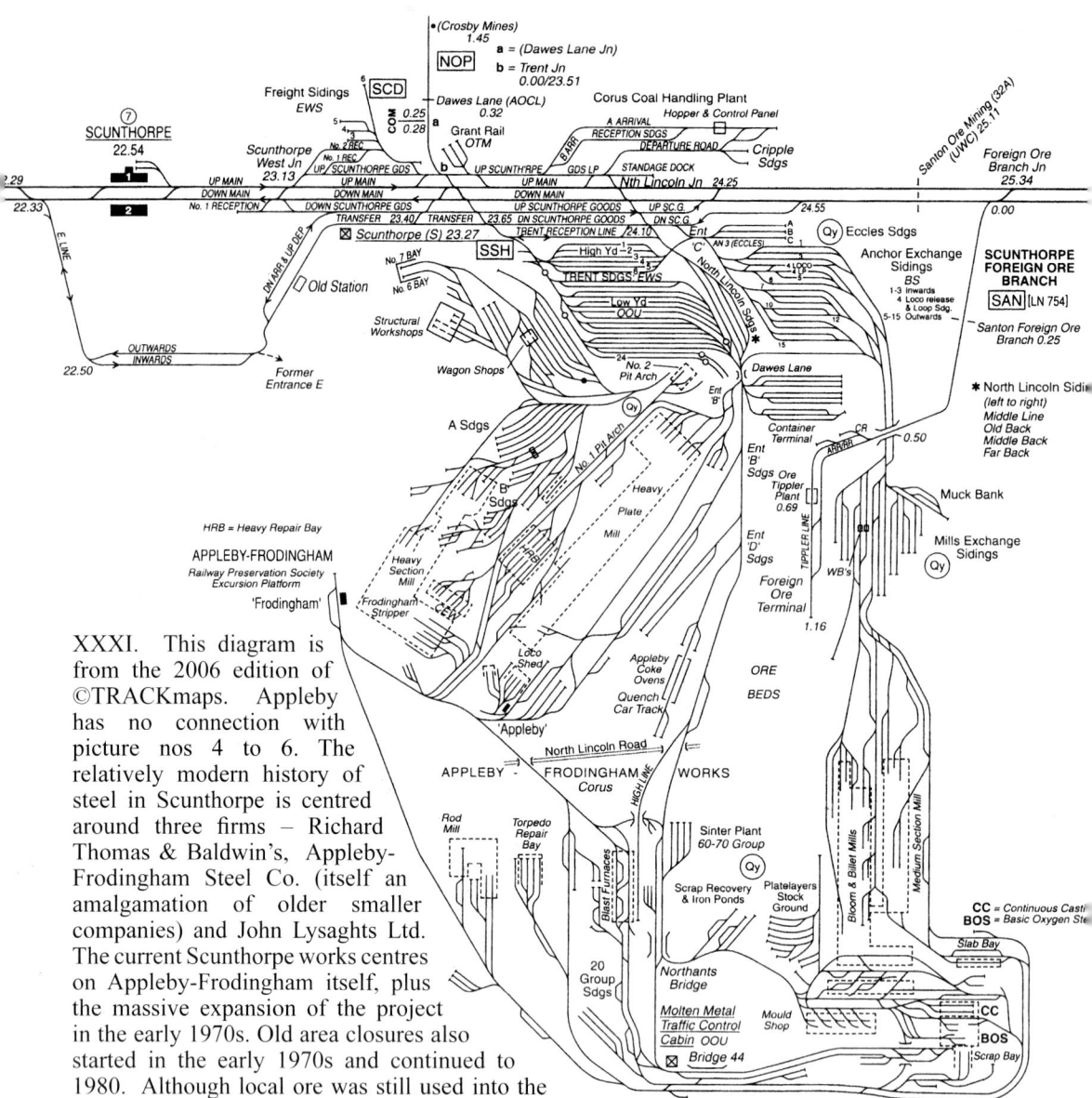

XXXI. This diagram is from the 2006 edition of ©TRACKmaps. Appleby has no connection with picture nos 4 to 6. The relatively modern history of steel in Scunthorpe is centred around three firms – Richard Thomas & Baldwin's, Appleby-Frodingham Steel Co. (itself an amalgamation of older smaller companies) and John Lysaghts Ltd. The current Scunthorpe works centres on Appleby-Frodingham itself, plus the massive expansion of the project in the early 1970s. Old area closures also started in the early 1970s and continued to 1980. Although local ore was still used into the early 1980s, all three companies shipped in iron ore from other places in the UK and later imported ore. The NLLR ended up as a BSC feeder line from Winterton and Roxby ore workings. One of the local traits was the use of the term Entrances for the various exchange sidings. Latterly these were Entrance A through to Entrance E, as shown here. The start of public railtours is shown on the left of the diagram and the platform stopped at for refreshments is smaller. It is shown above the words 'Appleby', near 'Loco Shed'.

XXXII. Private sidings were listed in 1938. By that time there were three main steel companies.

Scunthorpe and Frodingham ...	Crosby Building Estate Sid.	Scunthorpe Foundry Co. ...	Winn's Siding ....
Appleby-Frodingham Steel Co., Ltd.—	Frodingham Ironstone Mines	Sheepbridge Mine	Appleby - Frodingham Steel Co., Ltd.—
Appleby Iron Works	Glebe Mine	Sir Berkeley Sheffield's Sid.	Appleby Iron Works ......
Frodingham Works	Hydroprest Concrete, Ltd.	Tarmac, Ltd.	Bagmoor Siding ....
Steel Works	Lindsey Iron Works	Thomas, Richard, & Co., Ltd.—	
Beauchamp Mines	Lord St. Oswald's Mine......	Redbourn Hill Works......	Colsterworth Mine ....
Berkley Siding	Midland Ironstone Co.'s Sid.	Santon Brick Works	Cottesmore Iron Ore Mines
British Basic Slag Co., Ltd.	Normanby Mine	Trent Iron Works	Cringle Mines ....
	North Lincolnshire Iron Co.'s Siding	Urban District Council (Gas Works) Siding	Frodingham Works ......
Brookes, Ltd., Slag Works...		Wagon Repairs, Ltd., Siding	Glebe Mines ....
Buckley Bros.	Sandwith & Clugston	Ward, T. W., Ltd., Slag Works	Roxby Sidings..............
Chatterton Mine		Warren Mines	
Clugston, L. G.	Scott, Walter, Ltd., Iron-stone Mines		Steel Works ....
Conesby Siding	Scunthorpe & Frodingham Co-operative Society		

99. Redbourn Ironworks is seen in about 1880.
The two blast furnaces were charged from barrows
taken up the central lift tower. The blowing engine
house is on the left, near the wagons.
(R.Humm coll.)

100. We see Frodingham Motive Power depot's
new turntable pit in 1931. In the background is
Appleby Works. Caption 9 has the shed details and
no. 108 shows much of the yard. (R.Humm coll.)

101. The Redbourn Steelworks of Richard Thomas & Baldwin is shown with Hudswell Clarke 0-6-0T no. 13 on 11th April 1948. It is seen after its rebuild with inset cab and entrance to increase clearances in the Redbourn melting shop. (R.Humm coll.)

102. This is Appleby and the Frodingham Steel Company's Frodingham Steelworks on the same date. Seen here is Hudswell Clarke 0-6-0ST no. 1349 of 1918. It was rebuilt in 1946. Behind are believed to be some of the early cooling towers. (R.Humm coll.)

103. Here we see the United Steel Ore engine shed, with three 0-6-0STs awaiting work. Near the doorways are inspection pits between the rails. (Colour-Rail.com)

104. The Ironstone Mines Mobile Conveyor is probably the largest item to span beyond the standard gauge track loading gauge. Remodelling of Scunthorpe Yards took place around 1954. About 4000 wagons inwards and 4000 outwards passed through them each weekday and about 2000 in each direction on Sundays. (R.Humm coll.)

105. Clugston & Cawood Ltd, Lincoln Slag Works, is seen on 14th June 1952. Loco no. 2 is a Manning Wardle 0-6-0ST and it carries the owner's name. Originally no. 860 *Coppice*, it was built in 1893 for Coppice & Woodside Collieries, near Ilkeston. It was withdrawn in 1955 and scrapped by T.W.Ward in Doncaster. (R.Humm coll.)

106. A panorama from 21st May 1953 features class O4 2-8-0 no. 63626, a type introduced in 1911. The loco behind it appears to be hauling a train load of limestone; this aids steel production. On the right is the pre-1928 station building. (R.Humm coll.)

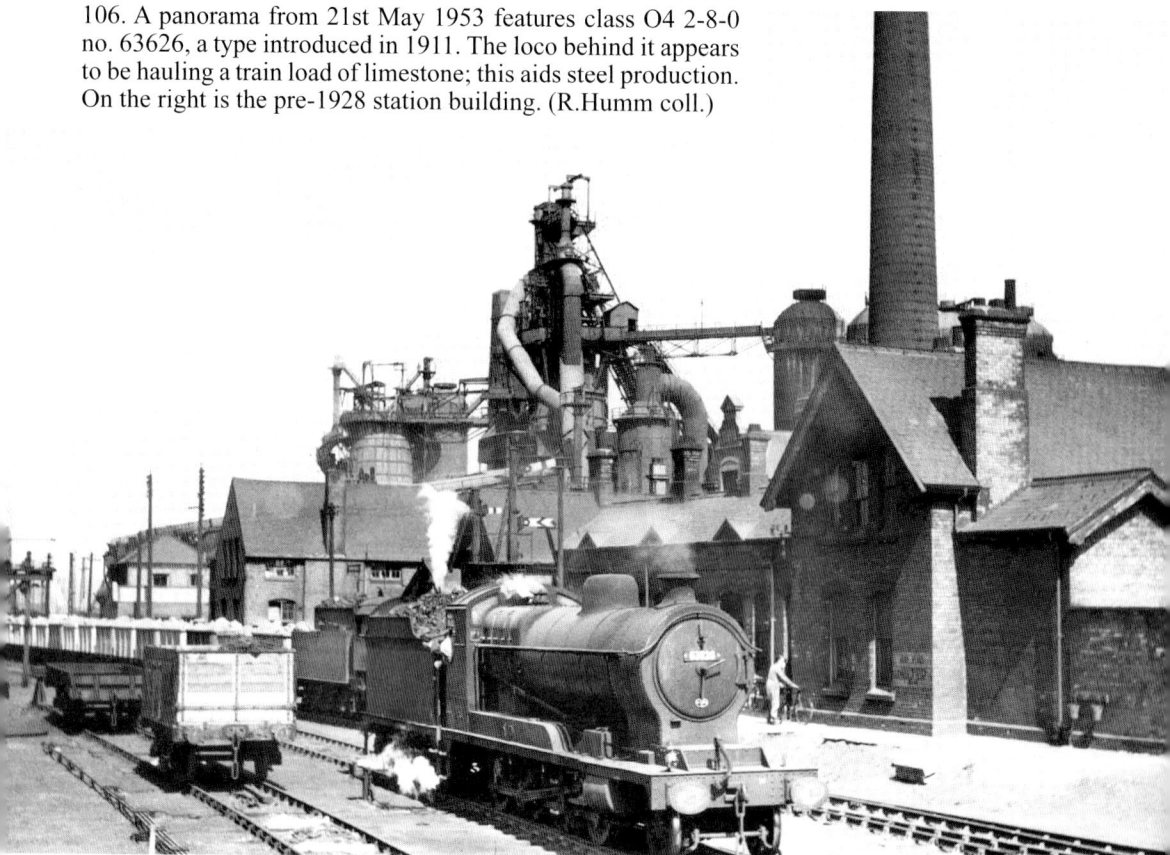

107. This fireless loco worked in the melting shop at Redbourn Steelworks on the site until 1965. Steam and boiling water was supplied by the works when needed. The loco was used for hot metal transfer work. (N.Fisher)

108. This is the motive power depot yard on 7th June 1960, with one long pit included. Parts of the steelworks are evident, while the engine shed can be seen in picture 9. It opened in 1932. Centre stage is no. 64404, a class J11 0-6-0, a type introduced by the GCR in 1901. See map XXV. (R.Humm coll.)

109. Yorkshire Engine Co. no. 2863 of 1962 was a 'Janus' class 0-6-0 diesel-electric locomotive with 440hp twin Rolls Royce engines. The locos were almost identical from both ends, hence the name, Janus, who was a 'two-faced god'. The engine is working at Appleby-Frodingham on 4th October 1976. This is typical Scunthorpe practice in the 1970s-1990s. It is working slag ladles south away from the main blast furnaces towards the slag tipping beds. (A.J.Booth)

110. This is fleet number 80, the eleventh and final 1124hp Hunslet machine, built in 1977. It is seen in June 1980 approaching Dragonby exchange sidings, with empty ore wagons heading north for refilling at Roxby. (R.Turner)

111. This is one of the former Normanby Park works main rail weighbridges. It was located at the bottom of the 'old route' near Dragonby Sidings. It is seen after closure in February 1981. The old route had been superseded by the 'new route' to the north to permit hot metal transfers. This route still survives as the connection to Flixborough Wharf. In the 1970s, it was used to service the Nypro plant there with tank wagon traffic. (R.Turner)

112. No. 18 was Bagnall no. 2762 of 1944, an 0-6-0ST. The view is from around 1960 and we witness an iron ore open cast working. In the distance is a loading dock and nearer is a catch point, due to the severe gradient. It is an early photo, as most of the train is made up of low capacity ore hoppers, with only one of the more modern ore tipplers. (R.Turner)

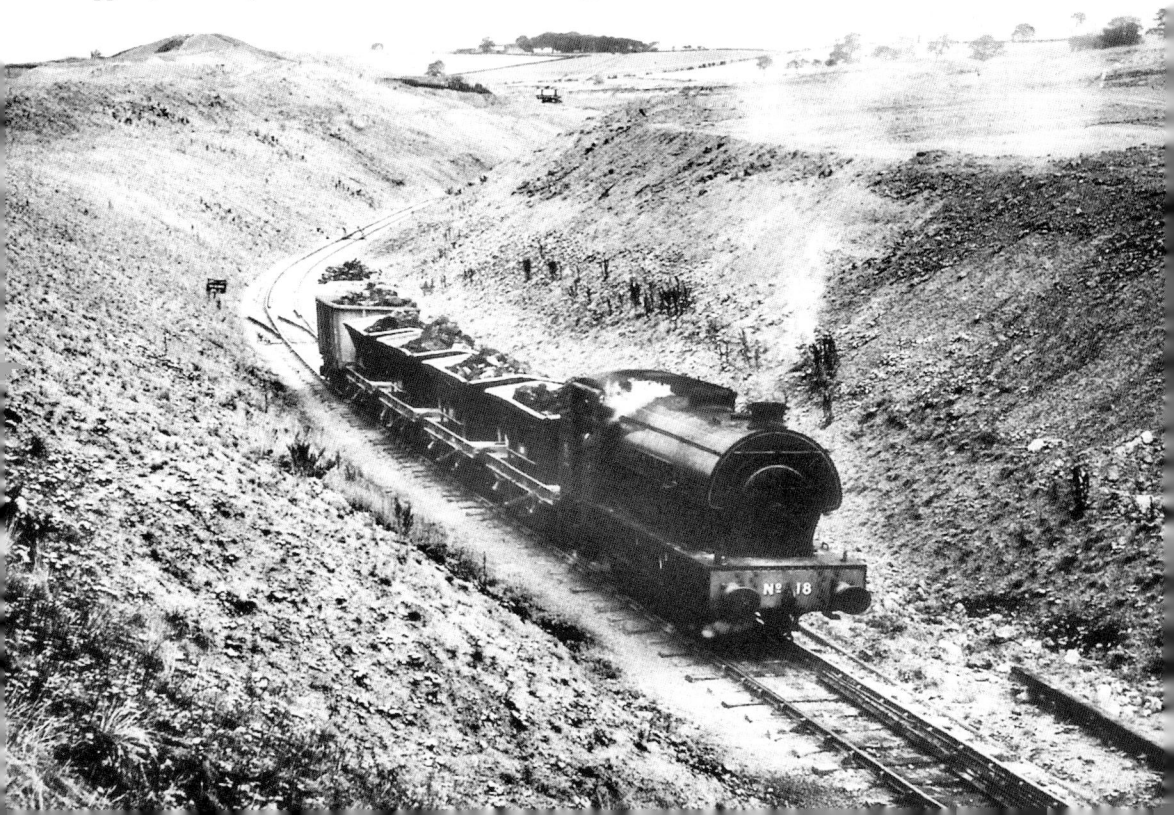

113. Nos 37252 and 37221 await their path on to the main line at Foreign Ore Branch Junction with empty iron ore tipplers for Immingham Dock on 13th April 1983. The main line can be seen on the far right, looking towards Scunthorpe station. The same iron ore tippler wagons were in use on this flow in 2019, but the traction was changed several times since the days of paired class 37s. (P.D.Shannon)

114. This is the 1958 Frodingham Traction Maintenance Depot just before its closure on 19th March 1993. It was north of the main line and the code was FH. Nearest on the left is no. 08508 and in the right background are parts of the steelworks. The site was taken over by GrantRail in 1999 and in 2004 the old depot building was demolished. A new depot was built nearby and was operated by VolkerRail (previously known as GrantRail) for maintenance of on-track machines and road-railers. (M.J.Stretton)

115. This is Dragonby sidings, the exchange point for Normanby Park works with BR, seen in February 1981. The locomotive is Hunslet no. 7473 built in 1976 and numbered 61. (R.Turner)

116. The Scunthorpe British Steel Works locomotive fleet was partially on view on 2nd August 1995. On the left is no. 76, one of the 1124hp Hunslet products, on lifting jacks. On the far right is another member of the class. No. 44 is a 'Janus' class, Yorkshire Engine no. 2768 of 1960. Half hidden by no. 76 is one of the seven Baguley Drewry/General Electric locomotives used only on the Blast Furnace's three elevated sidings, known as the 'Highline'. (Colour-Rail.com)

117. No. 66007 is arriving with coal on 11th April 2000. By 2018 there was just one Welsh coal train weekly. It was from Cwmbargoed, in South Wales. Most coal had been imported via Immingham Docks, for many years. (A.J.Booth)

118. We are in Appleby Depot on 9th July 2011. This is diesel-electric shunter *Arnold Machin*, built in 1958, by the Yorkshire Engine Co. with works no. 2661. Behind are some of the numerous gantries holding pipework which is conveying oils, gases, steam and water; with covered conveyor belts, far left and far right. Around 100,000 tonnes of rail for Network Rail have been produced annually by British Steel before the latter was declared insolvent in 2019, with 4500 jobs at risk. GB Railfreight had already begun hauling much of the rail stock to Eastleigh, regularly. (P.G.Barnes)

119. The location of this station is shown on map XXXI, the diagram near to picture 99. This and the next view are of the AFR on 1st June 2019. Two tour trains operated usually. The brake van one was hauled by 'Janus' class diesel-electric 0-6-0 No. 1; its journey length was about eight miles. No. 1 is Yorkshire Engine Co. no. 2877 of 1963. (V.Mitchell)

120. The second train was composed of a DMU driving car and a BR composite coach, pulled by an 0-6-0ST built by Avonside, works no. 1919, in 1924 and named *Cranford*. The coach tour was over about 15 miles usually and had a welcome detailed commentary provided. (V.Mitchell)

Other massive steelworks that are detailed in Middleton Press albums are both in Wales. Llanwern is in *Gloucester to Cardiff* and Port Talbot is in *Cardiff to Swansea*. Both volumes are in the Western Main Lines series.